BEMUSED

BY DIANE FINDLAY
ILLUSTRATED BY MARENA TUNKIN

This is for my grandchildren,
Connor, Kalee, Jordan, and Hayden,
and for Linda, who didn't get to hear all the stories,

with huge thanks to those who helped, especially
illustrator Marena Tunkin, editor Cecelia Munzenmaier,
graphic designer Michele Daves, Bob, Jan, Kelly,
Naren, Jordan, Emily, Shahla, Don,
and the Waukee Library Writers Group.

THE MUSES OF GREEK MYTHOLOGY

Polyhymnia (Pah lee HIM nee uh), "Polly": Muse of sacred music, geometry, agriculture, and storytelling
Thalia (THAL ee uh): Muse of comedy and pastoral poetry
Urania (Yew RAH nee uh), "Rani": Muse of astronomy and astrology, philosophy and religion
Terpsichore (Terp SIH kuh ree), "Chori": Muse of dance and creative movement
Erato (Air AH to), "Era": Muse of romantic poetry
Euterpe (Yew TER pee), "Terp" or "Sunny," here: Muse of lyric poetry and music, flute
Melpomene (Mel PAH muh nee), "Mel": Muse of tragedy
Clio (KLEE oh): Muse of history
Calliope (Kuh LI uh pee), "Calli": Muse of epic songs and heroic poems

THEIR PARENTS

Mnemosyne (Nem AH suh nee): A Titaness, whose name means "memory"
Zeus (ZOOS): One of the twelve great Olympians; ruler of the heavens, gods, and men

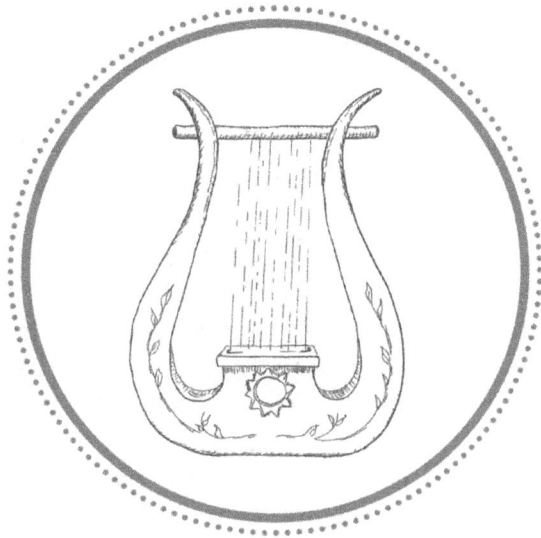

"Oh, Twerp, it's just like you to think that everything can be fixed with a little toodle of a flute!" Once again, Urania's serious nature bumped up against Euterpe's cheerful optimism. Talk had turned to Thalia's crush on Apollo, who didn't seem to notice her. But the subject hardly mattered, when it came to tension among the nine sister Muses gathered in the Music Hall. Despite the grand dimensions of their palace on Mount Helicon [1], they had been too much together in recent weeks, bored by the task of preparing yet another musical performance for yet another banquet. Any small thing might spark conflict.

"That's not true," Euterpe protested, "and it's 'Terp' to you, thank you very much! I only said that everyone knows the way to Apollo's heart is through music. How could he resist one of Thalia's funny little tunes? I don't hear you giving any better ideas."

Thalia sprang up and nearly upset Erato's harp in her

irritation. "Stop it, you two! Neither of you knows anything about this, so just stay out of it!"

"I know what I see," Urania retorted, pleased at getting a rise out of Thalia, who was lighthearted by nature and harder to rile than some of the other sisters. "And I see Apollo charming every pretty girl in sight, with barely a glance in your direction."

Thalia scowled, hands on hips. "Well then, you must be blind! Just yesterday he stopped and chatted with me far longer than he needed to, and told me I looked lovely. I'll prove it! I'll wager my serving of tonight's dessert that Apollo invites me to dance the first dance. And Athena's [2] here, busy in the kitchen. You know what that means!"

This rash bet took the others by surprise. Athena's desserts were high stakes indeed, and nothing to trifle with. Their voices rose in a cacophony of excitement and protest, speculation and scolding.

"**Enough**!" Mnemosyne's sharp, exasperated voice resounded as she swept around a pillar and into the hall.

The Muses were silent at once. They knew that tone. Their mother, usually patient with their squabbles, was clearly at the end of her rope.

"I have **had** it with your constant bickering! Morning 'til night, it never stops! I can't remember when I've had a moment's peace!" Mnemosyne's clipped footsteps echoed as she crossed the vast marble floor and paced before them. Her eyes flashed dangerously as she tossed her auburn curls. "You will stop this ungoddessly racket this instant, and not speak again until I've said my piece. Is that clear? **Just nod**!"

The startled sisters nodded in unison. Accustomed as the Muses were to getting their own way, even they knew to take heed when Mnemosyne was angry, and she was very angry now. A Titan [3] in her own right, Mnemosyne was tall, commanding, and used to being obeyed. And while she was fearsome enough on her own, woe to them all if she chose to call their father, Zeus, from Mount Olympus. His wrath could bring down the skies!

"I cannot listen to another minute of this wrangling!" Mnemosyne continued. "You need a break from each other and, Zeus knows, I need a break from all of you!" Regaining her composure, Mnemosyne seated herself on her ornate throne at the top of the hall, smoothed the folds of her shimmering gold robe across her lap, and straightened her jewel-encrusted crown. She let the tense silence linger. Finally, she spoke. "I've come up with a plan, one I don't believe you will take lightly. As you seem to disagree about everything else, what's at stake here will be the one thing you always agree about. Can you imagine what that might be? Anyone?"

With a graceful wave of her hand, Mnemosyne conjured up a mouthwatering, fruity aroma that filled the room. The fragrance, combined with the memory of their recent conversation, made the answer horrifyingly obvious to the trembling sisters. Calliope and Euterpe raised their hands in alarm. When their mother nodded in their direction, they gasped, in unison, "**Not** pear sorbet [4]?"

"That's it exactly! Since you all so covet your beloved sweet, you will meet my challenge or say farewell to pear sorbet—permanently!" Mnemosyne leaned back on her throne and let her words hang ominously in the air. "Now listen carefully. You will need to put all your quarrelsome energy into fulfilling my plan if you wish to succeed, and I'll accept no excuses. Are you ready to hear it?"

Nine sober faces with shocked, violet eyes nodded. For all their petty differences, the Muses were firmly united in their passion for the most heavenly delicacy of all. Life without pear sorbet seemed unimaginable!

"Good," Mnemosyne continued. "As Muses, part of your calling is to inspire mortals to achieve great things with their puny talents. It's time you got out there and did some inspiring! I will devise a mission of inspiration for each of you, and there will be not a single spoonful of pear sorbet for anyone until each of you has completed her task. Is that understood?"

Nods again.

Mnemosyne stood regally, folded her hands behind her back, and walked in a slow circle around her daughters.

"Your assignments will be in different countries to keep you out of each others' way. You will each help a young mortal of my choosing solve a problem or achieve a goal related to your individual gifts and talents. You may plan your strategy and fulfill your mission as you see fit. You may appear in whatever guise you wish, with whatever earthly skills or possessions suit your plan. But you will work with your young mortals **only** through ordinary interaction, and you will **not** reveal your true identity. I will assign your tasks tomorrow, one at a time, from youngest to oldest. Until then, you will remain in your separate quarters. You will appear only to perform one song at the festivities tonight, and then you will return to your chambers immediately. You will speak to **no** one. Understood?"

Again the Muses nodded, full of guilt and apprehension.

Thalia raised her hand timidly.

"Yes?"

"Are we allowed to help each other?"

Mnemosyne arched an eyebrow. "Well, now. I'm pleased to hear you admit that you might need one another. Let me think." She paused briefly. "After all your bickering, a large part of my purpose is to separate you. But how about this? You may meet with only one sister at a time, and you may not call for help more than twice during your missions. After all, you will each have your own work to do. You cannot be distracting each other or popping around the world willy-nilly. And remember—I'll be watching!" Mnemosyne glared directly into the eyes of each Muse in turn. "At the slightest hint of a quarrel, the offending sisters will forfeit and end the challenge for **everyone**! And that will mean the end of pear sorbet for all of you. Now go. Ponder your misdeeds and wait for my summons." Mnemosyne marched out of the hall, while her nine subdued daughters trudged silently to their separate bedchambers.

Early the next morning, Mnemosyne called Polyhymnia to her elegant sitting room. Polly hurried in, not wishing to anger her further. "Good morning, Mother," she mumbled.

An unusually cheerful Mnemosyne smiled with goddessly satisfaction at her own cleverness. "And a lovely morning it is! Now to the business at hand."

She handed Polly a parchment scroll. At the top, in

large, flowing script, were these words: "Your Mission, Should You Ever Wish to Taste Athena's Heavenly Pear Sorbet Again:"

Polly flinched to see the threat in print, but scanned the rest of the scroll for details of her mission. It was clear, specific, and daunting. She dared not complain. She nodded her head in acceptance.

"Now be off," said her mother. "As the youngest, you get a small head start. But don't waste time! You can be sure that the last Muse to finish her task will feel the impatience of her sisters, and we all know that's what got you all into this fix to start with!"

With a dismissive wave, Mnemosyne swept into her bedchamber while the youngest Muse made her way to the realm of the mortals.

One by one, each sister answered Mnemosyne's summons. Each received her scroll. And each set off to fulfill her challenge and inspire the actions of one humble, ordinary human like you and me.

Footnotes

1. Mount Helicon, south of Mount Olympus in Greece, is the location of the palace that is home to the Muses.

2. A little-known fact about Athena, famous as a goddess of war, is that she was also the goddess of wisdom and patron of crafts and practical skills, including homemaking and cooking. She was divinely handy in the kitchen.

3. The Titans, six brothers and six sisters, were the children of Mother Earth Gaia and the sky god Uranus. They were considered the first line of gods and goddesses, and were forces to reckon with.

4. Athena's pear sorbet, for anyone unfamiliar with this heavenly delicacy, is an icy concoction bursting with the rich, subtle flavors of the finest fruit to be found on Mount Olympus. You may, if you must, think of it as sherbet elevated to divine worthiness. It was Athena's heavenly specialty.

CHAPTER 2
THALIA'S MISSION: THE LAST LAUGH

Thalia, Muse of Comedy and Pastoral Poetry, you're off to rural Minnesota, in the land of America, where a young man longs to set his inner comedian free but suffers from a serious lack of confidence. Your task is to help him develop his talent and pursue his dream.

New Prague, Minnesota, USA

Timothy sprawled on the classroom floor, humiliated. It was the third time this week that Randall had managed to trip him up. *What did I ever do to Randall, anyway?* he wondered for the thousandth time. But he knew that wasn't the point. He was small. He was skinny. He was shy. He was a little geeky. To guys like Randall, that was enough. In sixth grade, big bozos like Randall picked on small nerds like Timothy. It's just the way things were. But he hated it, and he wasn't going to be able to take it much longer.

Wishing he were invisible, he picked himself up and made

6

his way back to his desk. Randall's smirk was predictable and infuriating.

When Timothy got home, his day went from bad to worse. His father sat him down and laid out Crunchy Munchies and milk, with an air of forced cheerfulness. Timothy frowned. This wasn't normal—his favorite snack, with zero nutritional value, without even asking for it? Something was up.

"Hey, Tim, there are some changes coming up that I need to talk to you about. You know the farm hasn't been doing so well lately," Dad began. The worried look that Timothy had gotten used to seeing on Dad's face returned. "People just aren't willing to pay extra for organic chickens now that the economy's so tight. I've found a job in Minneapolis, to keep us going until things get better. It'll come around. But for now, I'm lucky to find this job and I have to take it."

Timothy's jaw dropped. Hard as things had been, he hadn't seen this coming. "But, Dad, who'll take care of the chickens? And how will I get home from school on chess days?"

"Well, that's the thing. Joseph from next door can keep things going around here during the day. But with your mom working the evening shift at the hospital and me gone until eight most evenings, that's just too much time for you to be alone after school, not to mention the transportation issue." Dad forced himself to meet Timothy's eyes and took a breath before continuing. "So we've decided to find someone to be with you after school and take you places when you need to go. Your mom's looking for the right person to help you during those hours."

Timothy couldn't believe what he'd just heard. They couldn't mean... "No, Dad! You can't get me a babysitter! I'm eleven! What will people think? I can take care of myself! Please don't get me a babysitter! The money you save will help keep the farm going, right? Please!"

"I'm sorry, son." Dad's eyes were sad and Timothy heard real regret in his voice. "But it's already decided. I'm sure we'll find someone you like. The best way for you to pitch in is to make the best of it, and offer to help Joseph when you can."

"But..." Speechless, Timothy stormed off to his room. He

headed straight for the rug in his closet, where he hid away when he felt hurt or angry. Even at eleven, he found it hard not to cry. *Great*, he thought. *This is all I need. Randall's gonna love this! Now I'm not just Tiny Tim, I'm Tiny Baby Tim. He'll make me a laughingstock! I'm dead meat.*

The next day was Saturday. Timothy woke to the irresistible, buttery smell of pancakes on the griddle. Mom was making breakfast! He forgot to be mad, it smelled so good. He stumbled out to the kitchen, pajamas crumpled and coarse brown hair unruly, only to find a complete stranger standing there, deep in conversation with Mom.

"Here he is now! Good morning, Tim! There's someone I want you to meet." Mom was bubbly—too bubbly. Her voice sounded unnaturally eager. What was going on? "Thalia, this is Timothy. Tim, Thalia lives in Montgomery. She finished her high school credits early, so she's looking for a job to get her through 'til summer." The uneasiness in Mom's eyes clashed with her cheery tone. "She's going to spend some after-school time with you. I just know you two will like each other! It'll work out perfectly. I invited her for breakfast so you could meet."

"Hi, Tim! Nice to meet you." Thalia looked about seventeen, with long brown hair and a bright smile. Pretty. She was small, Timothy noticed, not much taller than he was, and dressed in jeans and a sort of tunic. She had the brightest violet eyes he'd ever seen. She stuck out her hand in Timothy's direction. "Your mom's been telling me about you and the situation here. I'm excited to get to know you."

Timothy was dumbfounded. *Who is this person? Where did she come from? How did Mom find her so fast?* His world was spinning out of control. He usually cracked a joke when he felt uncomfortable, but right now he couldn't think of a single funny thing to say. An awkward silence stretched out, punctuated by the sizzle of batter on the griddle.

"Uh, hi," he mumbled, leaving Thalia's hand hanging there, unshaken. "Um, I guess I'll go get dressed."

Timothy fled to the safety of his room to try to figure out a plan of counterattack. Things were moving way too fast. He didn't know if he felt more embarrassed about his appearance, humiliated to be treated like a little kid who needed a babysitter, or angry at his parents for messing with his world. One thing was sure—he did **not** want to get to know this strange girl standing all bright and cheerful in his kitchen.

But his stomach was rumbling and he couldn't resist Mom's pancakes forever. He pulled on some jeans, slicked down his cowlick, and made his way reluctantly back to the kitchen. While he stared at his plate and poured syrup on his pancakes, Mom caught him off guard with an apology.

"I'm sorry, Tim," she said, sinking into the chair next to him. "This must all seem pretty sudden to you. I forget that it was only yesterday Dad sprang the news on you. We've been talking about what to do for a while, but we didn't decide for sure until this job came up for him. It is all happening fast." She poured him a glass of juice and helped him to sausages. "But you'll never believe how I found Thalia—or rather, how she found us. It feels like it was meant to be. I was talking with Janine at work about needing an after-school friend for you, when Thalia introduced herself. She was at the hospital visiting her aunt and happened to walk by the nurse's station and overhear our conversation. I'm so glad she did! But I can see it's a lot for you to handle all at once."

Thalia jumped in. "I know I've just met you, but it feels like a good fit. I'm almost the youngest in my family and I always wanted a little brother. I drive, so I can take you where you need to go. And I think we could have some laughs. Do you like mini golf? I hear you play chess, and I'm not too bad at it. So how about it? See? No trick buzzer or anything." She extended her open hand toward him again.

What could he say? Much as he hated the idea, his mom was excited, this Thalia person was thrilled, and absolutely no one seemed to understand that he did **not** need a babysitter! Disgusted with himself for not having the guts to stand up to them, he shook her hand limply and admitted defeat. "Good to meet you, I guess," he muttered. *Still*, he thought, *she does know about trick hand buzzers. She can't be all bad.*

"Good! Then it's settled. More pancakes!" said Mom.

Breakfast went OK. *She's actually sort of fun,* Timothy admitted to himself, *not all bossy and full of herself like most kids her age. She talks to me like I'm a real person.*

As they compared experiences, Thalia said, "I think you're lucky to be an only child. I'm from a big family and the only way I get any attention is to make jokes and keep everyone laughing." Timothy's family was small, but he knew what she meant. When he accidentally sent sausage shooting across the table with his fork, she shouted, "Duck! It's a link bomb!" and giggled at her own wit. And it seemed like a good sign, when Mom went on and on about how great this would be, that Thalia caught his eyes, rolled hers, and winked. They had humor in common, anyway. It made him feel good to make people laugh. Maybe it was his talent. At least his parents thought it was.

His parents! They were the real traitors. He scowled at Mom, but he guessed he couldn't blame Thalia for taking a job when she needed one. Maybe it wouldn't be so bad. As long as they hung out at the farm, no one else had to know.

Timothy got off the school bus Monday afternoon hoping he was right about hitting it off with Thalia and no one finding out. He could sure use some laughs right now. Randall had bumped and baited him all day. There were no major incidents, but the pressure of knowing Randall was always there, always waiting for an opportunity, wore Timothy down. Preoccupied with his thoughts, he jumped at Thalia's greeting.

"Hi, Tim! Glad I beat you. It took a little longer to get here than I expected. How was your day?" She slowed down as she talked, taking in his appearance. His shoulders were slumped and his expression so hangdog that even his freckles seemed to droop.

"OK."

"Hmm… I'd never know it to look at you. You look as sad as a snowman in a rainstorm. Are you hungry?"

Instead of heading for his closet like he normally did after a tough day, Timothy let Thalia lead him into the kitchen. Over Crunchy Munchies (again!), they chatted. *She's funny and nice,* Timothy thought, *and she doesn't try too hard.* She asked him questions, but they were interesting questions; not too personal. They talked about the farm and how he helped out.

She didn't seem surprised, like lots of town kids were, when he said he liked living there, that the openness suited him, and the constant cackle of the birds was sort of nice. She asked what he liked to do for fun and he found himself telling her about his love for comedy. Pretty soon they were laughing and trading jokes. He loved puns; she favored blonde jokes.

"How do you keep a blonde busy for hours?" Thalia asked. "Give up? Give her a piece of paper with 'See other side' written on both sides! I tried that on my sister Mel once, and it worked, for a while, anyway!"

She had a funny little charm on her key ring that Timothy said reminded him of "the hook" they use to drag lousy performers off stage [1]. She got a kick out of that.

"You're funny, kid. You need some original material, but your timing is good. You're a natural. We can work on your delivery, if you want," Thalia offered.

"Work on my delivery? You mean really practice the funny stuff? What do you know about it?" Timothy asked, eyebrows raised.

"I told you I'd been making my family laugh all my life. But I also got some training last summer, learning stand-up comedy at the Pantheon School of Performing Arts out East. It was a blast! It would be fun to share it."

"That's so cool!" Timothy grinned, feeling better than he had all day. His crooked smile made it all the way to his greenish-blue eyes. "I really want to learn. I think I want to be a comedian when I grow up."

"Really? Have you written any of your own stuff? Show me what you can do!"

"What? Now? But I haven't... No, I couldn't," Timothy stammered. "Actually, I have a lot of homework. I should get started. I might need some help with my math, though. Do you know anything about math?"

"Not really; I never liked it much. You know what they say: A math teacher is someone who talks in everyone else's sleep!"

By the next week, Timothy and Thalia had developed a routine. Timothy came home from school and they chatted, joked around some, went out to collect eggs and pick vegetables for dinner. Timothy did his homework. He didn't mind so much. It was strange not having his father there when he came home. But Thalia was OK. He didn't feel shy around her and she seemed to like spending time with him.

They tried to "out-funny" each other. "Hey, Tim," she'd say. "What do you call a brunette with a blonde on either side? An interpreter! (Trust me, it's true—I've been there!)" He'd counter with, "Did you hear about the dairy farmer who couldn't get his prize cow to give milk? It was an udder failure." But they kept it short, not like real comedy routines. That would feel too much like performing, and Timothy just couldn't get his nerve up for that.

On Thursday Thalia met him at the bus, car keys in hand, and reminded him that he had a dentist appointment in town. "I'm glad I got here on time. I got sidetracked by one of my sisters. She needed help with a project. Anyway, drop off your stuff and let's go," she said. Timothy headed for the truck without a second thought, even though it was the first time they'd gone anywhere together. It felt just fine, right up until he bit his lip on the way out of the dentist's office.

"Ouch!" he yelped, dripping blood and stinging, in spite of the Novocain the dentist had used. Thalia laid an arm across his shoulders in sympathy as they walked back to the truck. And who should come by on his bike just then, and see Timothy in his weak moment, being led across the street like a baby? Randall, of course.

"So, Tiny Tim! Did ya get a owie at the dentist? And who's this? Got a nanny to take care of you and change your diapers? Ha!" Randall pedaled off gleefully.

"Who was that awful boy?" asked Thalia. "Not a friend of yours, I hope. You know the old saying, 'With friends like that, who needs enemies?'"

"Nobody! Just leave me alone," Timothy growled, through teeth as clenched as they could get, under the circumstances. He shook off Thalia's arm. He was fuming. Seething. Mad at Randall, at his parents, even at Thalia. Most of all, he was mad at himself for letting his guard down. Now he was in for it. Randall would be relentless, making the most of this new ammunition.

He was grateful that Thalia did, at least, have the good sense to get them in the truck and out of town, and not try to talk about it. They headed straight home.

Back in the kitchen, as the numbing chill of ice cream soothed his sore mouth, Timothy began to calm down. Thalia gave him time; she didn't bug him with questions. Even when she complained that the ice cream was a poor substitute for some fancy treat she had at home, she kept looking at him with an eyebrow cocked in concern. When she finally sat down and asked about Randall, Timothy let himself tell. All of it. How he'd always been shy, but felt really alone since his friend Connor moved away last fall. How Randall was just always **there**, waiting to taunt and humiliate him. How he didn't even mind the bruises so much, but more how Randall made him feel small. And how much he wished he had the nerve to stand up to him.

Thalia took it all in. For once, she didn't joke. When he was done he felt a little better, just for letting it all spill out. They were quiet for a while. Finally, Thalia broke the silence. "I just made it worse for you, didn't I, by helping you to the car."

Timothy heard the concern in her voice. "Probably," he said. "But it doesn't matter. It's not about anything you did, or even anything I do. It's just the way it is."

"You know, kid, you're not only funny, you're pretty smart for your age. You're a joker, not a fighter. It's not your style to puff up like he does and fight back. And you shouldn't have to." Thalia sat back and thought for a moment. "Maybe we can figure out a way to use your strengths to disarm him."

Timothy shrugged, but he was listening.

"For starters, how about this?" Her face brightened a little, now that a plan was forming. "When he starts bugging you about a babysitter, tell him I'm your cousin. Cross your fingers behind your back if you need to. I don't think a little white lie will do any harm."

"I don't suppose he'd believe you're my girlfriend," Tim suggested with the hint of a smile. "That might shut him up for a while!"

"I'm a little old for you, don't you think?" Thalia flashed a smile of her own. "But there are things we can do. We can work on using your humor to show him he's not getting the best of you. Bullies back off if their victims don't give them the satisfaction of being embarrassed and scared. Maybe you can be funny, instead."

"Funny? He already thinks I'm hilarious! He makes jokes about how I look like an elf and smell like chickens. He says I'm such a loser my best friend moved away! He's full of one-liners, and when he's around, I've got nothing."

"Wait a minute." Thalia sat up straighter, excitement in her eyes. "I think Randall may have something to teach you about being funny. Have I told you the three rules of comedy?"

Timothy shook his head.

"Well listen up, 'cause here goes," Thalia announced, raising one finger at a time. "Rule #1: Use what you know. Make jokes about yourself, your life, your experiences, things going on around you. Rule #2: Keep to the point. You can draw out a punch line a little, if you know you've got your audience's attention, but don't take side trips—set it up, and then get there. And Rule #3: Have a heart. Mean jokes aren't funny, even though people might laugh because they're uncomfortable. People who resort to mean jokes are pathetic and desperate. I'll bet you know that one already, because of Randall."

"True," Timothy acknowledged. "But there's nothing funny about my life. What's funny about gathering eggs and spreading chicken manure on the vegetable garden?" His shrug made him look skinny and defeated.

"Maybe more than you think. You'd be surprised how much humor you could find in your life out here. There's a funny side to almost everything. You just have to look for it and figure out how to use it. And, Timothy, please!" Thalia punched him lightly on the arm. "Lighten up a little! Call it 'chicken poop!'"

"But how can any of that help me with Randall? And how can I fight back with jokes, if I can't even use mean ones? **He** doesn't worry about 'having a heart.'"

"Good point. But here's what I'm thinking. If you let other

kids see your funny side more, it might help you find a buddy or two to walk around with. Bullies aren't nearly so quick to pick on kids in groups as they are on loners. My oldest sister Calli can be an awful bully, but even she backs down when the rest of us stick together. I remember one time…"

Realizing her talk of home was losing him, Thalia got back to the situation at hand. "Anyway, let's work on it, OK? How about this: You're in the cafeteria and school lunch looks particularly disgusting. What could you say to the kid next to you to make him laugh about it?"

A slow smile spread over Timothy's face. Almost an hour of serious comedy work later, he realized with a start, "I have homework!" But the two had laughed so hard, and come up with such great material, that he couldn't help hoping things might get better. Armed with a small repertoire of jokes about school lunches and pop quizzes, teacher impressions, and more, he headed to his room with a little spring in his step.

In the weeks that followed, the strategy seemed to work. When Timothy compared the mashed potatoes and gravy over noodles on his lunch tray to an albino tarantula, kids actually laughed and a couple of guys invited him to eat with them. When he wore his T-shirt with a picture of the Jolly Green Giant on the back and "Promote Whirled Peas" on the front, one of the popular girls said it was cool and asked where he got it. Unfortunately, Randall was not amused. Somehow, every well-received joke, every friendly chat, every companionable walk down the hall that Timothy enjoyed seemed to make Randall madder. He glared meaner, shoved harder, and jeered more often than ever. It was the cloud over Timothy's growing sunshine.

The next Tuesday, two things happened to tilt Timothy's precariously balanced world.

First, Thalia met him at the door with a big smile on her face and a sheet of paper in her hand. She gave it to him. The heading read, "Le Sueur County Amateur Hour Variety Show! Come and show us what you've got!" Right below that was his name filled in on the top line of the application form, followed by "Comedy routine." Timothy looked up at her, bewildered. She started speaking in a rush.

"Before you blow a gasket, kid, I haven't already signed you up. I need your signature for that. But you're ready! I know you can do this. It's the perfect chance to try out your new material in front of an audience. It's a variety show, so you won't be up against a bunch of other stand-up comics—maybe only one or two others on the program. It's county-wide and in Montgomery, so you'll have a fresh audience, not just people who know you already. This is it—time to let your light shine!"

Thalia's sales pitch was so earnest, so convincing, that Timothy startled himself by saying, "I'll think about it." He wasn't making any promises, but he couldn't quite make himself say no, either. By the time they heard Dad's car tires crunch in the driveway later in the evening, they had agreed to keep it between them and talk more the next day.

The second tilt happened later, as Timothy and Dad reviewed the day over dessert. Timothy was preoccupied with the thrilling, rather alarming secret of his possible comic debut, and almost missed his father telling him that they would have visitors on Thursday. "Ted Thompson's in charge of a fancy dinner for some state bankers' convention, and he might buy chickens from us. He wants to see our operation, so I'm taking a couple hours off work to come home early and meet with him. This could be good for us!" Timothy saw a glimmer of hope in Dad's eyes that he hadn't seen in a while. "He mentioned that his son would be with him, since it's a school in-service day. Isn't his son in your class, Tim? Maybe you can entertain him while we talk business."

That grabbed Timothy's attention! *Banker Ted Thompson's kid? In my class? Randall's last name is Thompson! He brags all the time about how his dad's a rich banker. Oh, no. This can't be happening! Randall here, at the farm? And me, expected to pal around with him while our dads talk shop?* He couldn't think of anything worse! And while Randall probably couldn't pound him with both of their dads nearby, he'd make life as miserable as he could and use everything he saw to fuel future attacks. For a moment, Timothy saw the farm, which felt so comfortable and friendly to him, through Randall's eyes—the old-fashioned farmhouse, laundry on the clothesline, slightly weedy garden, rusty utility tractor in the yard, and the squawking, messy chickens everywhere. Randall had managed to intrude on his private world and ruin this day, when Timothy almost felt good enough to agree to perform, without even being present!

"But Dad, I think we have an extra chess meeting that day," he blurted, desperate to avoid what felt like being a lamb led to slaughter.

"I don't think so, Tim. The school paper said no extracurricular activities on no-school days. Besides, I need you here. You wanted to help? Keeping Ted's son occupied will be a big help."

It was futile to argue. Timothy knew this contract could help put the farm back on its feet. Resigned to his fate, he said goodnight and trudged off to bed to dream about his miserable life.

He was no cheerier when he got off the school bus on Wednesday. In fact, his gloom had turned into anger, and Thalia was the handiest target. "Forget it!" he snapped, before she could even mention the Variety Show. "I'm not doing it! It's pointless and stupid and nothing you say can make me!" He stormed into his room, slammed the door, and headed for the closet.

Thalia dropped into a chair and scrunched her brow. *What's this?* She'd expected Timothy's insecurities to resurface before he agreed to perform; she thought she could tease him out of that. But shouting and slamming doors was unlike anything she'd seen in him before. She'd thought she was making progress! *What now?*

When Timothy refused to come out for supper, Thalia knew she needed help. *OK,* she thought. *Don't panic. Time to call a sister. Which one? I need someone who understands fear and courage and perseverance. Maybe Clio, the Muse of history! It takes serious determination to wade through all that history—the heroes and the cowards, the rises and the falls. And, Zeus knows, she can wear all of us sisters down! Maybe she can help me get through to Tim.*

Thalia slipped into the bathroom. She tapped out the

sisters' secret code on her fingers—one tap to the left ring finger, since Clio was the second-born sister, followed by one tap to the right middle finger, telling Clio that she, the eighth-born sister, was calling her. Almost before she finished, Clio materialized next to her.

"Couldn't you have found someplace a little roomier?" Clio complained. "I might as well be sitting on your lap!"

"Nice to see you, too, Clio."

"Right. How's your mission going? Not great, I guess, or I wouldn't be here."

"Of course, not great," Thalia snapped. "No need to rub it in! I just don't know what to do." Calming a little, she filled Clio in. "Timothy has real talent—he cracks me up all the time. He's a natural performer. But this bully's smashing what little confidence he has. Now he's angry at me, and I don't know how to get through to him. He's really a pretty cool little guy. How can I convince him to take his chance in the spotlight?"

"Hmm... History's full of bullies and cowards, as well as heroes," Clio pondered. "But sometimes the tables get turned. Even Hector ran for his life when Achilles charged him [2]. Sometimes bullies turn out to be cowards and sometimes cowards surprise everyone by turning into heroes. If your kid is worked up enough to be mad, maybe a little reverse psychology will push him through it and make him use the anger to raise some gumption. Psych him out by doing the opposite of what he expects. Discourage him. Tell him he's not up to it, and see how he reacts."

"Really? Do you think it'll work?"

"Why not? What have you got to lose? The clock's ticking on all of our missions, and you've got to do something. I say give it a try."

"OK. I don't have any better ideas. Joking and coaxing aren't going to work this time. Thanks!"

"No sweat. Don't mess this up! Here's to pear sorbet, all around! Have you tasted what passes for frozen dessert around here?" And with that, Clio was gone.

Thalia made up a supper tray and tapped on Timothy's door. "Tim, I have supper for you. Can I come in? I promise not to push you anymore about the talent show."

Timothy's eyebrows arched in surprise. He'd expected Thalia to try to joke him into a better mood and then do just that—push him to perform. When she didn't, he was a little disappointed. And truth be told, he was hungry. He shoved the door open with his toe and let Thalia in. "Alright then, but don't even try. I'm not doing it, and that's final."

"OK." Thalia took it all in—the sad face, the slumping posture. Even the vague, pleasantly musty boy smell she'd gotten used to seemed pathetic and her heart went out to him. Suddenly she needed to do this. She needed to find a way to help him. She took a breath and plunged in. "I've been thinking, anyway. I don't know. Comedy's a tough business, kid. Maybe you're just not cut out for it. I guess I was wrong to push you, just because you've got some talent. I'll throw away the application." She picked it up from his desk and tossed it in the wastebasket. "Enjoy your supper." She ducked out, hoping she'd managed to bait him just enough.

What? That's it? She's giving up on me? She thinks I can't handle it! She thinks I'm gutless! Something inside him swelled up, big and strong and a little unnerving. Almost of itself, Timothy's body acted out his growing anger by storming around the room upsetting everything within reach. He tore back the covers on his bed, kicked his backpack, and swept the chess set off his desk. *OK. So maybe I have been gutless. But who is she to tell me I'm not cut out for the one thing I'm good at? I'll show her! I **will** perform in the Variety Show, and I'll knock 'em dead! That is...* he thought, suddenly deflating as he remembered the doom hanging over him tomorrow, *if Randall lets me live that long. I may be in no shape to knock anyone dead by then.*

Timothy's tantrum ended as suddenly as it began. He crawled into bed, miserable and confused, and drifted into a restless sleep.

"Nice farm you have here, Mr. Carlson," Randall gushed as the boys and men walked from the driveway past the porch and toward the poultry house.

"Why, thank you," replied Dad, looking pleased.

Timothy gagged at his tormentor's phony politeness

around the fathers. Randall almost managed to sound like a normal kid! But the first chance Randall got, he shot Timothy a "just you wait" smirk that dispelled any hope of the day going well. When the fathers sent the boys off to "play," Timothy's heart sank. They left the poultry house. As soon as they were out the door, Randall started in, shoving and teasing.

"Bawk, bawk, bawk! Gee, Tim, I'll bet all your little chicken brothers and sisters really look up to you! They sure look and sound like you. Smell like you, too." He was just winding up when Thalia appeared.

"Hi, guys! You must be Randall. I'm Tim's cousin Thalia. Come on in the house for some cookies." She led the way. The minute she showed up, Randall switched back into "impress the grown-ups" mode which, while disgusting, was still a welcome change. Timothy knew that Thalia was as curious to meet the infamous bully as she was eager to be hostess in his mom's absence. But he was grateful, just the same. Even after her betrayal of the night before, she felt like an ally with Randall around.

The route back to the house led right past the vegetable garden, where Timothy had just dumped a fresh layer of fertilizer from the chickens. Even he flinched at the potent smell, made even stronger by last night's rain. The boys were a step or two behind Thalia as they approached the garden. Timothy could see Randall's nose wrinkle at the same time his eyes lit up with evil intent.

It happened so fast that Timothy wasn't sure about the sequence of events. One minute Randall was positioning himself to "accidentally" push Timothy into the garden. And the next, Randall was lying there, face down in the muck, with Thalia standing over him, all apologetic concern. "Oh, Randall, how could I be so clumsy? I'm so sorry! Are you OK?" As she pulled Randall to a sitting position, Timothy got the shock of his life. Not only was Randall as totally, sickeningly, gloriously covered in chicken poop as he had intended Timothy to be, but his face was streaked with tears! The dreaded Randall was crying! Thalia made a show of helping him up and ran to the house for towels.

Timothy couldn't help it—he really couldn't! He began to

laugh. He laughed so hard that he cried, too. He didn't even care if Randall pounded him. He knew it didn't matter what Randall did to him from now on. This moment was worth it all! He would always have this picture in his mind, and Randall would know just what he was thinking. There might not be many perfect moments in life, but this was one!

As Randall awkwardly wiped the trace of tears from the coating of filth on his face, he tried, unsuccessfully, to muster an air of menace. "Chicken boy, you'd better **never** tell anyone about this, you hear me? If you ever tell, I'll knock you into next week!"

Timothy was laughing too hard to reply, but he managed to stifle himself just as Thalia arrived with an armful of towels and effusive offers to hose Randall down. Randall grabbed a few towels, sputtered a very rude refusal, and stomped off toward his father's car. Timothy and Thalia watched him go. The sight was so pathetically hilarious that they only had to glance at each other to set off a bout of uncontrolled giggles. Thalia tried to be serious. "Maybe we shouldn't be laughing. He really is miserable, you know."

"He sure is! Isn't it great? Trust me; he had it coming, and more. How did it happen? He meant to push me into the poop. He was getting ready to do it when he fell. Oh my gosh— Thalia! You didn't..."

"Well, I might just have happened to step back right at that moment. It's vaguely possible he tripped over my ankle."

They went off in gales of laughter again, both knowing they would never say another word about it to anyone. It would be their delicious secret, and Timothy's powerful secret weapon against future bullying.

After that, Randall's power over Timothy evaporated, and they both knew it. Relieved of one fear, Timothy focused on his remaining fear—trying out his comedy in front of a real audience.

The school year was almost done. Soon Thalia wouldn't be coming over anymore. *I'll miss her*, he realized. She hadn't said anything more about the Variety Show, but he was sure she hadn't forgotten. He couldn't get it out of his mind. Maybe he should really do this, partly as a thank-you to Thalia, but mostly for himself. When would there be a better time?

A week before the show, he handed her the signed form, which he'd recovered from the wastebasket. She grinned and hugged him. "OK, kid. Let's polish your routine. I think you need to focus on the farm life stories. They're your best bits."

The auditorium was packed. The lights dimmed. Timothy felt sick to his stomach. He didn't know if the strangers, Thalia, or his family and neighbors made him more nervous. *I can't do it! I have to do it!* And he had two acts ahead of him to endure the agony. *Maybe I'll just die and get it over with!* But then he thought of the headline in the County newspaper: "Young Would-be Comic Gives New Meaning to the Phrase 'I'm Dying Here!'" He couldn't help smiling a little. Maybe it would be OK after all.

Disoriented by the lights and the crowd, Timothy stumbled onto the stage. He started stiffly, with an "udder" joke that fell flat. But then he realized he liked the sound of his voice amplified by the speakers. He took a deep breath, gathered all his courage, and launched into his routine, feeling the beginnings of exhilaration: "I live on a chicken farm. Now you might think there's nothing much funny about gathering eggs and spreading chicken poop on the vegetable garden. But it turns out, you'd be wrong...."

Thalia, sitting in the front row with muscles knotted and breath held, sighed, exchanged smiles with Timothy's parents, and sat back to enjoy the show.

Footnotes
1. Thalia is often pictured holding a comic mask and a hooked shepherd's staff. The charm Timothy sees is a way for Thalia to keep one of her signature symbols close to her.
2. Hector was recognized as the greatest Trojan fighter in the Trojan War, unrivalled for courage and nobility. But when Achilles, the mightiest of Troy's Greek enemies and enraged at Hector for killing his best friend in battle, attacked him, Hector's

survival instincts kicked in and he fled. While Hector eventually faced Achilles, the Greek's ruthlessness and rage prevailed, and Hector was slain.

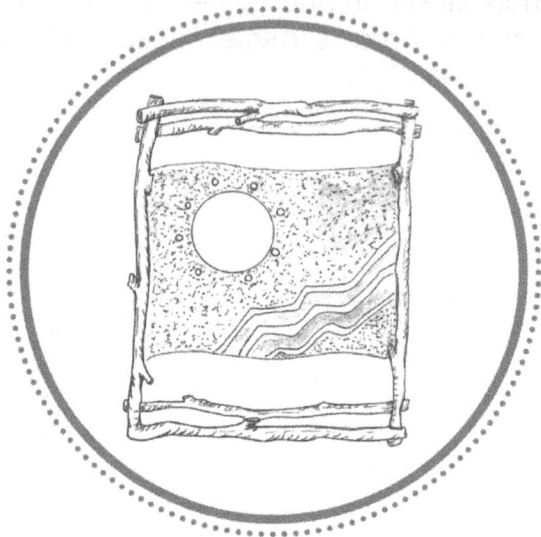

CHAPTER 3
POLYHYMNIA'S MISSION: THE GEOMETRY OF HAPPINESS

Polyhymnia, as Muse of sacred music, geometry, and agriculture, you're going to the Outback in Australia. You'll meet a girl with a passion for geometry, who just moved from the city. She's bitter about the move and blames her parents. She needs to discover the potential for developing her gifts in her new surroundings. Your task is to help her find a way for her talents to bloom along with happiness in the Outback.

The Outback near Alice Springs, Northern Territory, Australia

Pirra looked up from the boxes she was helping her parents unpack. She'd been homesick since the minute they left the city. But now, holding a book about the Sydney Opera House, she felt tears trickle from her brown eyes, down her cheeks, to catch in her long brown hair. Her muscles tensed with the effort not to give in to sadness and anger, but she simply couldn't contain them.

"I hate it here!" she exploded. "Why did we have to leave Sydney? There's nothing here, just a bunch of cows and sheep and wild animals."

Her mom sighed. "Oh, Pirra, we've been over this so many times. This job with the uranium mine is too good for your dad to pass up. It's a career-maker. We'll all miss the city, and it might not be forever. But for now we need to make the best of it and look for the good things here."

Dad tried to hug Pirra, who stiffened in his arms. "I'm sorry, honey. I know it's hard, especially for you. But it could be really great, too. I mean, look at all this amazing nature and wide-open space! Some people dream their whole lives of being able to explore the Outback...."

"Out back is right—out in the middle of nowhere! There's nothing to do and nobody to do it with!" Pirra threw down the book, ran to her room, slammed the door, and fell sobbing onto her bed.

Her parents looked at each other in dismay, but let her go. They'd only been here a few days, and hoped that it would just take some time for Pirra to adjust. But it hurt to see their daughter so unhappy.

Polyhymnia sat in a small shed on the back section of a tidy farmstead, shielded from the main house by a stand of scrubby trees. The shed was light and cozy. A little creative use of her goddessly powers had turned it into a pleasant little home away from home. She suspected Mother had given her an extra nudge, directing her to this exact location. She nodded with satisfaction.

But what now? In this very remote part of the world, where she knew no one and had no ordinary means of transportation, how could she connect with the girl who was the subject of her mission? What could she tell Pirra Morgan about who she was and what she was doing here, in a place where people in general, let alone girls Pirra's age, were scarce? She could hardly just appear, unexplained, from nowhere. The more she thought, the more she came up empty. *I need a plan, and I'm not getting anywhere on my own. Too bad I can't just have Pegasus [1] carry me around! Do I dare call a sister already? What if I need more help later? I'll only have one more chance to ask.* Still, she was stumped. *OK, which sister?* Polly's mind went immediately to Urania. *Rani understands patterns—where things are and how they move and affect each other, as well as how people think. She's imaginative, but not frivolous like some sisters I could name.... She should be able to help me form a big-picture strategy.* Polly tapped out the code on her fingers and was soon joined by her dreamy, bookish sister.

"Polly! Already? I've barely gotten my own mission! Any earlier and I'd have still been waiting for my turn with Mother. Doesn't all of this make you nervous?" Urania asked. "I don't know whether to be excited or horrified by the whole thing! So, what do you need? Let's make it quick. I've got my own planning to do."

"Planning is the point, Rani. I'm here, but I don't know how to begin. This place is so big and there are so few people! I need help figuring out how to explain being here at all, let alone guiding my girl in the right direction. Who should I be here? How do I fit in? How do I even get around? What do I tell Pirra about what I'm doing here?"

"Slow down! One thing at a time. But I see what you mean. Your cover story may be trickier than for some of us. Let's start with what we know. How far from here to where your girl lives?"

The two sat on the floor, head to head, reviewing the facts.

"I'll bet you're right, Polly. I think Mother steered you to this spot as a hint. You said the old couple that owns this place keeps to themselves, right? So maybe it's safe to use them as part of your cover. Could they be grandparents that you're visiting? But so busy with something of their own that you can make excuses for not involving them? And how about a bicycle? That would at least get you to where Pirra lives, and give you some exercise, too."

The beginnings of a plan took shape. There would be risks and Polly would have to be careful. But it was a place to start. She hugged Rani. They wished each other luck, and Urania was gone. Polly admired the shiny purple bicycle that appeared next to the shed. *Yes, this is just right.* After walking it around the trees so as not to be seen from the house, she pedaled down the dusty road toward the tiny post office and general store about five kilometers of the way between home base and Pirra's house.

Several days later, Polly visited the post office for the third time. It had proved an excellent place to eavesdrop and learn about the area, under the guise of running errands for her reclusive "grandparents." Mrs. Harris, the postal clerk, was a shameless gossip and knew everyone. Polly's heart raced. It was Thursday and a fresh batch of mail was in from Alice Springs. Someone from Pirra's family was bound to show up. She stood by the magazine rack, thumbing through teen magazines and hoping she wouldn't have long to wait. She didn't.

"G'day, Mr. Morgan!" Mrs. Harris called to a tall man entering the shop. "There's mail for you from Sydney."

That must be Pirra's father. Here we go! Making sure Mr. Morgan was within earshot, Polly asked the clerk if she knew of any kids her age living nearby. The man looked her way eagerly as Mrs. Harris waved him over. "Here's someone you should meet, young lady."

Mrs. Harris made the introduction and the two shook hands and chatted briefly. Luckily, Mr. Morgan was so concerned about his daughter, and so happy to meet a potential friend for her, that he asked Polly little about herself. In minutes, she had accepted an invitation to lunch on Saturday. Assuring Mr. Morgan that she could get there on her bike, she headed back toward the shed, whistling all the way.

"Guess what!" Dad announced at dinner that evening. Pirra scowled at his enthusiasm, while her mother beamed, already knowing what was coming. "I met a girl about your age who's here visiting her grandparents, just a short way down the road. She's looking for friends too, so I invited her over on Saturday for lunch and the afternoon. How about that? She seems very friendly."

Pirra, torn between interest and irritation, let irritation win.

"You committed my time without even asking me? That's not fair!"

Dad countered, "Look, you've complained and complained about not having other kids around. How many chances like this will come along? Was I supposed to let her walk away without saying anything? Really, honey, you need to give her a chance."

"But she's a total stranger! I don't know anything about her. What will I do with her for a whole afternoon? What if I don't like her? How will I get rid of her?"

"Just give it a try, sweetie," Mom cajoled. "Maybe you'll have lots in common. She doesn't know anyone here either. At least you can do each other a favor and spend some time together."

"Oh, alright. I don't have much choice now, anyway. It's just one lousy afternoon and I don't have anything better to do."

Despite her annoyance, Pirra found herself watching the clock all through the long, slow Saturday morning. When the knock came at 11:45, she worked hard to look bored as she ambled past her parents to open the door. It was rainy and cool outside. Pirra's fist impression was of a walking rubber raincoat, which hid most of her guest's slight body. Atop the rain-slick coat, Polly's auburn hair, braided around her head, dripped and sagged sadly. Polly was, altogether, a bedraggled-looking specimen. *Great,* thought Pirra. *Like it or not, this is my new best friend. It could be a very long afternoon!*

Dad hurried to bring Polly inside and make introductions. Mom fussed over Polly, taking her wet gear and placing a steaming cup of tea in her hands. She noticed Polly's bike in the yard and apologized for not picking her up.

"Thanks, but I really didn't mind the ride. It's wet, for sure, but I'm enjoying the exercise and the open spaces. At home, I almost never have a chance to get away by myself. It's one of the things I like about being here."

Pirra watched Polly chat with Mom. The girl wasn't so odd-looking without the rain gear. Sort of interesting-looking, in fact, with dimples that showed when she smiled. And her eyes! Pirra didn't think she'd ever seen eyes that color before—almost purple. Polly wore purple leggings and old-fashioned boots with an oversized, oatmeal-colored sweater. The combination suited her striking coloring.

Over lunch, Pirra's parents asked Polly questions about her home, her parents, and grandparents. Polly answered briefly and turned the conversation away from herself with questions about the Morgans. *Interesting,* thought Pirra. *She's almost as good as I am at dodging parental nosiness, and she's not one of those people who can't stop talking about herself. It's too much to hope that she likes math, but maybe this won't be so bad, after all.* By the end of the meal, all Pirra really knew about her guest was that her parents were touring Europe and she seemed bafflingly excited about being stuck in this God-forsaken wilderness with a couple of old people who were busy writing a book and had little time for her.

When the girls went to Pirra's room to get acquainted, Pirra apologized for her parents. "They mean well, but they can't seem to help prying into everybody's business—especially my friends'. So you must be an only child, too?"

Polly hesitated. She didn't know how much to share of her real story, and was afraid of tripping herself up with too much detail. But, truthfully, she was enjoying the time alone and was exhilarated by the chance to make up a new identity for herself. Impulsively, she muttered, "You could say that." *It's not really a lie,* she rationalized. *I didn't say I **am** an only child, just that you could say that. You can **say** anything!*

"But all that stuff about being happy to be here," Pirra went on. "Don't you feel like you've been dumped here while your parents travel? There's nothing to do here! I'd hate it if my folks did that to me! Wouldn't you rather be exploring London or Paris?"

"Not at all. They said I could go with them. But I've been there before, and I'd rather be here. This is such an adventure, and so different from most of the places I've been." *Well **that's** the truth,* Polly thought to herself.

"Well, I think it's awful! What's interesting about living in a desert? What about concerts and art museums? How do you make friends when there are no other kids for kilometers around? Some kids here have to do their school work entirely on the computer. How sad is that?"

Polly was thinking about how to turn the conversation in a positive direction when her eyes fell on an amazing picture hanging on Pirra's wall. It was black and white, and showed four panels of figures gradually changing shape from left to right. She jumped up to take a closer look. The picture was titled *Metamorphosis*. "This is fantastic! It's pure geometry," she raved, bouncing with excitement. "I've never seen anything like it!"

Pirra was stunned. Lots of people liked M.C. Escher's work. *But "pure geometry?" Could it be?*

"It's M. C. Escher. Haven't you seen his art before? What do you mean by 'pure geometry?'" she asked, barely daring to hope for the answer of a kindred spirit.

"Just look at it!" Polly replied. "It's all about shapes and how they relate to each other in space. That's pure geometry!"

"Wowzer," Pirra whispered. "Don't tell me you're a math nut, too! I love math! I was part of a competing math team at my school in Sydney. And I love Escher's work. I saw a whole traveling exhibit of it in Sydney. But it's the geometric pieces that really excite me. Are you into math, too?"

"Absolutely! I've been good at geometry my whole life. I'm kind of known for it at home. It's one of my favorite things. But my si... I mean, most of the people around me at home don't get it at all. I'm so glad to meet someone who loves this stuff, too! Tell me about your math team."

The afternoon flew by as the two talked animatedly about tangrams, pentominoes, and Fibonacci numbers. Pirra showed Polly a book with more of Escher's work. They shared tricks and shortcuts for calculations. *She knows her stuff,* Polly acknowledged. *Not as well as I do, of course, but enough to impress me.*

After describing a particularly satisfying Mathletes victory, Pirra's demeanor suddenly changed. She dropped onto the bed, shoulders slumped, and hung her head. "You can bet there won't be a Mathletes team meeting online or running off to competitions out here. Or exhibitions of Escher's art, either."

Her voice quivered as the sudden ache overtook her. "I guess that's all behind me now."

Polly gaped at the transformation. She could feel Pirra's sadness, and with it, the enormity of the challenge she faced. No simple encouragement would work here! The losses Pirra felt were huge and real. Polly scrambled for words that didn't sound empty.

"Maybe not. We can do lots of geometry things while I'm here. We can make up challenges for each other. We can look at Escher's art and find other geometric art in books and online." Polly hoped she didn't sound as floundering and desperate as she felt. "And we can do other stuff—find interesting things to do around here. What else do you like to do? What did you do with your friends in Sydney?"

"Oh, lots of things!" Pirra perked up at the memories. "We'd go to the Opera House, visit museums, go to dances, hang out at the Youth Club, order pizza, picnic in the park, visit the beach.... You can't do any of those things out here!" The excitement that touched Pirra's voice and eyes fizzled out at the end.

Being with this girl is like riding a griffin [2]—all dips and dives, so you're never sure which way is up! She needs to even out before she'll be able to think about new possibilities. Polly considered for a minute. "Maybe we can find out from other kids what there is to do around here. My Grandpa told me their neighbor on the cattle station has a son a little older than us. Let's see if we can meet him. We could ask him to show us around the station. I'd love to see how a big ranch works, wouldn't you? And he could tell us what kids do for fun here."

Pirra responded gloomily, "Hmm, I'm all for meeting other kids, but touring a cattle ranch doesn't sound like a very exciting way to spend a day."

"Come on, we can make it fun! Don't you like animals? Besides, what have we got to lose? It's not like our social calendars are full."

"My friends back home would never believe I'm planning a day with a bunch of bawling cows for entertainment," Pirra sighed. "How pathetic! But what else have we got to do? I give

31

in. When do you want to go?"

"Let's try for tomorrow afternoon. Maybe your mom could help us set it up and give us a ride. I know the boy's name."

Mom was thrilled to help—anything to encourage Pirra's interest in, well, **anything** in this new place! One phone call and it was all set. Mowan Taylor would meet them at the house at Pine Creek Station on Monday.

Polly was tempted when Mrs. Morgan offered to drive her and her bicycle home, but she decided not to invite questions. Her thoughts raced as she pedaled back to the shed on roads that were, at least, less muddy with the return of sunshine. She'd wanted to see the cattle station ever since she heard about it at the general store. *Now if this boy who lives there isn't a complete dud, maybe I'll be on my way to success!*

Cheered a bit by finding a friend and making some plans, Pirra spent Sunday unpacking and setting up her room with less resentment than before. Meanwhile, Polly took long walks, enjoying the surprising pleasures of solitude, nature, and even the tantalizing sense of danger as she thought about shaping and protecting her fictional identity.

Monday morning, the Morgans' truck stopped at the top of the road where Polly said she'd meet them. ("No need to go all the way down the dusty drive to the house.")

"All set?" asked Mrs. Morgan.

"Let's go," Polly answered.

At Pine Creek, Mr. Taylor and a boy who had to be Mowan greeted them. Father and son looked much alike. Both were medium height, with skin that looked like leather—wind-scoured and suntanned. Both wore jeans, boots, T-shirts, and wide-brimmed felt hats. Both had ready smiles that lit up their eyes before showing on their mouths, making them pleasing to look at, if not exactly handsome. Mowan looked nothing like the young men Polly was used to at home. Sure, many of them were muscled and handsome, but they lacked Mowan's ruggedness and unselfconscious confidence. *Who says the gods have everything?* she thought. The adults headed inside for coffee and a visit before Pirra's mom left the girls for the day.

Mowan laughed when he heard Pirra's name. At first she frowned, taking offense, but he quickly explained. "Your name—you know it means 'moon,' right? In the old Aboriginal language? I'm just laughing because my name means 'sun.' Moon and sun, right? What a pair! Too bad Polly doesn't mean 'stars' or something!"

Mowan's friendliness put the girls at ease and the three set off to see the compound. Mowan answered Polly's questions about the family garden and the cattle operation. But Pirra wasn't interested in any of that, so conversation quickly turned to teen social life.

"Don't you go mad with loneliness and boredom out here?" Pirra asked. "I mean, no offense, but all this empty space and no one to talk to but cows—I don't know how you stand it."

Mowan chuckled. "Actually, the cattle can be pretty good company. At least they don't give you a hard time like two-legged company can. But you're right. Even though I'm used to it, it gets lonely." He grinned at them. "I'm glad you came here today. It's nice to talk to someone close to my age. I have friends not too far away, and now that I drive I get to see them more. But it's not like hanging out at school every day or getting up a ball game at a moment's notice. We're too far apart and I have too many chores. We're lucky to get a cricket match together once a month. Even then, it's likely to be all ages, not just kids."

Just then Pirra noticed the unusual necklace Mowan wore. A ceramic figure of concentric circles anchored four strands of leather that formed the rope. "What's that?" she asked.

"It's an old Aboriginal design. The circles stand for a place of rest, so I keep it with me when I'm working the cattle. They don't give me much chance to take it easy!"

"Look, Polly. It's beautiful. And it's 'pure geometry,' like you said about the Escher print."

Polly stepped in close to study the symbol. "It sure is—both beautiful and pure geometry. Mowan, you said your name is Aboriginal. You knew what your name and Pirra's name mean in the Aboriginal language, and you wear this necklace.

Are you Aborigine?"

"No, we're European transplants through and through. But I sort of wish I was. I was born here. My parents were impressed with the way the Arrernte [3] people lived with the land around here for such a long time—thousands of years. So they gave me an Arrernte name. I admire them too. I'm interested in their traditions. I especially like Arrernte art. A lot of the designs are like this," he continued, tracing the curves on the pendant with his finger, "using simple shapes to mean different things. Sometimes, when I can get away, I volunteer at a museum of traditional arts in Alice Springs. I like the people there."

Pirra's eyebrows shot up. "A museum? Around here? What's it like?"

"It's small, but nice. I'm sure it's nothing like you're used to in Sydney, but I like it. Bigger isn't always better, you know," Mowan chided gently. Then he turned to Polly. "What about you? I know you're not an Aussie, but I don't recognize your accent. Where are you from?"

Polly nearly froze up, torn between trying to keep her story simple and the pleasure she felt in reinventing herself. "Well, actually, I've moved around a lot. I was born in Greece, but now I live in Spain," she blurted out. *Spain? Where did that come from?* "I guess my accent is a mix of lots of things."

Pirra jumped in excitedly. "You live in Spain? I didn't know that! You have to tell me all about Madrid! My friend's brother goes to college there and says it's full of great museums and stuff to do!"

Luckily for Polly, the trio found themselves back at the house and she was able to change the subject. "Thanks for the tour, Mowan."

"Oh, that's just the pre-tour." Mowan jerked his thumb over his shoulder at a group of four-wheelers parked along a corner of the house. "Now for the real tour."

"What? On those?" Both girls' eyes widened.

"Of course. How else could I show you the cattle? I get the idea that livestock doesn't excite you, Pirra, but Polly seems interested in the real business of this place. Right, Polly?"

34

"Definitely! But I've never even ridden on anything like that, let alone driven one."

"Me, either!" Pirra agreed.

"Then it's time you learned. You can't spend time in the Outback without experiencing life on a quad bike! You'll love it—it's a rush!"

"I don't know, Mowan." Polly was nervous. "It looks kind of dangerous."

"No worries, we have helmets. Come on, I'll show you."

Mowan was a good teacher. Within half an hour, the three were careening across the fields, squealing and gasping for breath. Pirra had to admit to herself that she'd never done anything like this in Sydney. Polly's braided hair came loose and felt wonderful flapping in the wind. The three ended the afternoon as friends, with plans to get together the next week.

"I'll show you some Arrernte crafts and we can take out the quad bikes again," Mowan promised.

The girls chatted excitedly the whole ride home. When Pirra admitted that she hadn't been bored all day, the relief on Mrs. Morgan's face was obvious.

Fantastic! thought Polly. *Pirra's already coming around and I can't remember when I've had such a good time! To think I was worried. This is going great! I can't wait for next week. I wonder what Mowan really thinks of us. I wonder what he thinks of me….*

On Tuesday, Polly and Pirra sat watching a movie in Pirra's living room. The movie was disappointing, so the girls talked through it. Conversation turned to Mowan and Pine Creek Station.

"So, Polly, were you honestly interested in those awful cows, or was it really Mowan? Do you think he's cute?"

"Of course I'm interested in the cattle! I'm not one of those silly boy-crazy girls like so many of my si... I mean like so many girls I know. I've always been interested in animals and growing things, and especially ways to grow food that respect animals and the earth. Sorry if that sounds preachy, but it's important to me."

"Whoa, I didn't mean to hit a nerve," Pirra commented,

eyebrows raised. "Just asking. You don't seem boy-crazy at all. Pretty serious, in fact. I'm not the boy-crazy type, either. It's just hard for me to imagine anyone being drawn to those big, noisy, messy critters."

"Sorry. People tell me I get too serious sometimes." Polly's brow wrinkled and her finger rested on her lower lip as she tried to explain. "It's funny. Being here, with space and free time and new experiences, I actually feel less serious, somehow. I think about all the same things I did at home, but I feel freer here. As for Mowan, I know lots of guys who are more handsome, but he seems so nice and, really, he's not bad to look at, either. What do you think of him?"

"I like him a lot, but not like a crush. I had a crush on a guy on my math team back home and I guess I'm not over it, though that hardly matters now that I'm here." A frown crossed Pirra's face, but she managed to shake it off. "Mowan feels comfortable, like he could be a real friend. So if you like him, go for it! That wouldn't bother me at all."

"I don't know. I won't be here very long and I'm no good at flirting. Not nearly as good as my si..." Again, Polly caught herself tripping over her own lie.

Pirra looked at her strangely. "OK, that's the third time you've started to say something that sounded like 'sisters.' What's going on? Are you an only child or not?"

Oh, dear, I should have known better! I'm just not a good liar. I should never try to pretend—I can't pull it off. But I can't tell the whole truth, either.

Thinking fast, she came up with what she hoped was a convincing save, with a little truth sprinkled in. "OK, here's the story. My parents aren't together. I live with my mom, but I have a bunch of sisters that are my dad's kids. Some of them are really annoying; some are OK. But they think I'm boring because I'm more serious. They don't get the agriculture thing at all, or the math. So that's why I'm so glad to find a friend who loves geometry, too." Polly glanced sideways at Pirra. *Will she buy it?*

"Wow, that's got to be strange. Do your sisters live in Spain, too? Do you see them a lot?"

"Yes, I see them often. I even sort of miss them here,"

she commented, surprised to realize that it was true. "So, tell me about this guy on your math team."

"Wait a minute. You said your parents were touring Europe. Does that mean you have a stepdad?"

"Oh, right. A stepdad. Yes. He's a pretty good guy and he makes Mom happy."

As the conversation took a safer turn, Polly thought, *Whew! That was too close. Note to self: From now on, watch the lies and don't dig yourself in deeper!*

Saturday found the girls back at Pine Creek. After a rousing ride on the quads, Polly, Pirra, and Mowan leaned against an old tree, catching their breath and drinking from canteens.

Polly turned to Mowan. "You said you volunteer at a museum in Alice Springs. What do you do there?"

"Different things. Sometimes I show visitors around. Sometimes I help in the art studio. Sometimes I sweep or carry out the trash. Whatever they need."

"Art studio?" Pirra's eyes showed surprise. "Do they have classes there? Do you actually make art?"

"Don't sound so surprised," Mowan countered. "Aboriginal art might not be the manliest of hobbies, but I figure I have the manly part covered working out here. I do like playing around with my own art using the old symbols and traditions. I'm not very good at it, but it's fun to try. Mostly, I'm an extra pair of hands in the classes, to help the young kids."

Polly was intrigued. "Do you have things you've made here? Will you show us?"

Mowan looked at them quizzically, as if deciding something. "I don't usually show people my art. Honestly, most of my friends aren't that interested. But I'm not sure anyone's actually asked before. Why not? I work on it in that little building back by the house. Tell you what—I'll race you back. If either of you beats me, I'll show you my private studio!" He wiggled his eyebrows teasingly and took off for the quads.

Of course, Mowan won the race. But he agreed to show the girls his studio anyway. He hesitated a little as he opened the door to the dusty shack and led them inside. "This is it. Not exactly a fine art gallery, but it's all mine."

On the walls hung sculptures made of bits of metal, wood, stones, and molded clay. They all featured simple geometric shapes like those in his necklace. There were spirals, waves, u-shapes, and more concentric circles. There were triangles, squares, and rectangles. Wavy, irregular lines connected softly rounded shapes, all finished in natural metal and earth colors.

"Mowan, these are amazing!" Both girls moved along the walls to study and touch the primitive but graceful assemblages. Mowan hung back, embarrassed and pleased.

"They're nothing special, just something I play at. But I like doing it."

"I think you're too modest," Polly scolded. "They really show the beauty of natural things and suggest a time when people cared more about the earth."

"And look, Polly," Pirra said excitedly. "These have that same 'pure geometry' we've been talking about."

"I don't know much about math," Mowan said, "but I know my friend Lark at the museum talks about something like 'sacred geometry' in the traditional arts. You should meet her! She'd love it that you're into the geometry of it all. Let's go to Alice Springs next week. I'll show you around. We can visit the museum. Maybe you can meet some of my friends there. I'd love to see my mates and I really think you'd like Lark."

"That sounds great!" Polly clapped her hands at the thought of another adventure and realized, though the other two had no idea, how well her mission was going. *This isn't hard at all! I wonder if the other sisters are having as much fun as I am.*

"Mowan, how many people live in Alice Springs?" Pirra asked, with a little edge of her earlier resentment in her voice. "It's barely a spot on the map, right?"

Mowan nudged her playfully. "Sure. For a city girl like you, Alice will hardly feel like a bump in the road. But it has its charms. And it's the closest thing to a city you'll find around here, so you might as well get used to it."

For a moment, Pirra felt bad for what Mowan could have taken as an insult to his world. But he was so good natured about it that she let it go and laughed at herself. "OK, you're right. Considering that two weeks ago I thought there couldn't be one good thing about this backwater, and now I have a couple of friends, new experiences to tell people back home about, and some actual plans, I guess I should expect to be surprised. Maybe even in a good way!"

Lunch at a sidewalk café in Alice Springs with three of Mowan's mates had been fun. Even being chased inside by a sudden rain squall added to the pleasure of what was a surprisingly interesting day so far. Polly enjoyed Mowan's easygoing style. His friends were nice, too. Quint was a little rough around the edges for Polly's taste, and Dar was shy. But Kalee was smart and funny, with an independent, breezy style Polly envied. If she seemed a little too glad to see Mowan, Polly could hardly blame her. Pirra and Kalee connected immediately when Mowan mentioned that Kalee was the leading brainiac on her school's academic bowl team. By the end of lunch, Kalee was campaigning for Pirra to move to Alice to fill a gap in math strength on the team.

"What do you think of Alice Springs?" Mowan asked Pirra as they strolled through the Cultural Precinct toward the Mbantua Art Gallery and Cultural Museum, dodging the last of the raindrops.

"Well, Sydney it's not!" Pirra laughed. "But you're right; it has its charms. I like your friends, Mowan. I wish I could show you and Kalee Sydney," she continued, wistfully. "You'd love it! It would be such a blast. But for now, I have to admit that this is nice too, in a quaint, old-fashioned way."

"Higher praise than I expected," Mowan nodded.

"Mowan, is Kalee your girlfriend?" Pirra asked.

Mowan's face colored. "No, nothing like that. I mean, maybe she could be if I saw her more. But she doesn't think of me that way. She's just a good friend. And now for the highlight of the tour," he said, changing the subject. "I have a feeling you two and Lark are going to go off into geometry world and forget I'm even here!"

They entered the small, but light and modern, gallery. A tiny, dark-skinned woman with star-bright eyes, who had obviously been waiting for them, scurried over and wrapped

Mowan in a motherly hug. "Werte [4], my favorite cattle rustler! How are you, atyewe [5]? It's been too long between visits!"

Mowan hugged the woman back. "It has, atyewe! I've missed you. The rainy season means more work on the station. But I had to come today. I have some new friends that need to meet you. Lark, meet Pirra and Polly. They're both staying near the station. I think you three have some things in common."

"Well, that's intriguing. Tell you what. I have to meet with a man about a grant. You know how it is, Mowan, we're always chasing after funding around here! You show the girls around. Make sure you look at Lindsay Bird's new work. It's one of the best collections we've shown. I'll find you when I'm done. We'll sit down with a cup of bush tea and see about these 'things in common.'" Lark scurried off down a hallway.

Bird's paintings fascinated them, with their range of colors from deep earth tones to primary brights, their repeating patterns, and always, everywhere, geometry. They eagerly read wall text and pointed out interesting symbols and patterns to each other. "See, Mowan," Pirra teased, "I guess this guy doesn't think art is unmanly. Not many men do batik paintings like these, but look where it's gotten him. And see that photo? He looks plenty manly to me!"

Polly, who'd been as caught up in the artwork as the others, suddenly felt her heart sink. She sat on a bench with her finger on her lip. *This is going way too fast,* she thought. *At this rate, Pirra will have her happy future all wrapped up in no time, and I'll be whisked back to Mt. Helicon to take up my role as the boring, serious Muse the others tease or ignore. I'm not ready to give up my bicycle and my windblown hair and my new friends—especially my new friends! But with Mowan and Kalee and all this geometric art, Pirra's doing great. She hardly needs me at all anymore.*

"Polly, what's up? Are you OK?" Pirra sat next to Polly and put a hand on her shoulder. Mowan joined them.

"I'm fine. I'm just a little homesick, I guess. It's like you said, Pirra, this place is so small and out-of-the-way, compared to Rome or Madrid or Sydney. I know you miss Sydney, too."

"I do. I really do. But it's not so bad here, after all. What happened to all that excitement about adventure and new experiences? I never thought I'd be the one cheering **you** up and trying to convince **you** about the good things here! Besides, you'll be going home pretty soon. I'm here for... who knows how long?" Pirra's shoulders sagged as her words reminded her again of all she'd left behind.

Pirra's moodiness sent a brief wave of satisfaction through Polly, followed quickly by guilt. *Not cool, Polly!* she scolded herself. *I can't let myself forget why I'm here. No matter how much fun I'm having, I have a job to do. Besides,* she realized, *Pirra really is a friend. I can't feel good about making her feel bad.*

Mowan stood by, feeling uncomfortable with them for the first time, as he tried to take in this roller coaster of rapidly shifting female emotion. "So where's Lark when you need her?" he mumbled.

As if on cue, Lark strode into the gallery and swept them into her orbit with her enthusiasm. "Well, that went well! I think we have a good chance at a grant for an exhibition we've been trying to book. Time to celebrate and get to know these new friends of yours, Mowan."

Over strong, slightly bitter tea in the staff room, with their shared interest revealed, Lark launched into a lively introduction to the concept of sacred geometry—geometric forms and symbols in nature and indigenous art. She was so earnest and so delighted at their interest that she drew Pirra in instantly. Polly tried to resist, not yet ready to let go of her worries. But Lark's enthusiasm was too contagious; she gave in. Even Mowan, who claimed to understand not a word of the math, could relate to the idea of symbolic shapes and patterns in nature. Lark sketched designs and symbols, lecturing casually. Pirra grabbed a pen and sketched, too, to illustrate her questions.

"Pirra, have you studied art?' Lark asked.

"Not seriously. I've taken a few classes. But I really like art—especially this stuff! It just makes sense in my head. It seems to come out from my fingers through the pen without even thinking about it. This makes me want to try it and see what I could do. Have you seen Mowan's art, Lark? He says he's just playing at it, but I think it's really good."

"No." Lark reached over and tousled Mowan's hair. "Mowan hasn't seen fit to show me his work. I'd like nothing better. I've seen what he does when he helps around here, and it makes me suspect that his own art might be something special."

"No fair ganging up on me!" Mowan laughed. "Besides, we should get going. It's a drive home, and I have to be there to help Dad later. And if I hear much more talk about planes and polygons and acute angles I think my head will explode!"

"Alright then, if you must," said Lark. "But I have an idea. We just got permission from the city for a public art project. We're going to work with local children to paint a mural of Aboriginal designs on a building near here. But we'll need lots of help to keep the kids corralled and on task, let alone learning what we hope they'll learn. Why don't you three come and help? We're starting soon, and we could sure use you." Lark winked at the girls. "Maybe we could even sneak a little math in there when they're not looking! There's room on the mural for your designs, too. Even just for a couple of days? You could stay at my house so you don't have to drive back and forth. What do you say?"

Pirra's eyes sparkled. "What do you think? Could we, Mowan? I'd love that! I've seen lots of public art in Sydney, but I never got to make any."

"I guess I have no one but myself to blame," chuckled Mowan. "I knew you three would be dangerous together! I don't think I could stay over this time of year, but I could probably come for a day and bring the girls. What about you, Polly? Are you in?"

"I'm in," Polly replied. "At least as long as I'm here," she added glumly, remembering that the better things went for Pirra, the sooner she'd be gone.

That evening Polly paced her tiny cottage, thoughts tumbling over each other like players at leapfrog. *OK. It's good that things are going well. My job is to help Pirra find ways to let her talents bloom and feel good about being here. Right? Check! She's not nearly so homesick. She's met people she likes and found fun things to do. She's not only found ways to use geometry, but she's expressing it in art. Bonus! And it hasn't even been hard. Am I done? I can't be done already. Maybe that's the catch! This is too easy. What if she's only OK because I keep pushing her to go places and do things? Mowan is busy with the station and her parents can't take her to Alice all the time. Maybe if I leave she'll get stuck right back where she was. Maybe she'll be even more frustrated because she knows what she's missing. If I go back too soon, it could all fall apart. I can't let that happen. Just a while longer…*

Polly nearly jumped out of her skin when she turned and saw Urania standing across the room, looking none too happy.

"Rani? You nearly scared my hair white! What are you doing here? I didn't call you!"

"No, you didn't." Urania glared at Polly. "Mother yanked me away from my own work to come here and straighten you out! She didn't explain, other than to say that you keep almost blowing your cover. Just that you were getting yourself in too deep and needed a nudge. So tell me." Urania sighed and sat on the bed, recovering from her annoyance. "What's going on with you?"

"I can't believe Mother did that! Is she really watching that closely? Yes, I had a little trouble keeping track of what I told Pirra about myself, but I've fixed all that. I don't need help. Actually things are going very well…." Polly filled her sister in, sharing the thoughts she'd been chewing on before Urania's arrival.

"… So you see, I need to stick around and make sure that Pirra works with Lark and gets to know Kalee better and spends time with Mowan so it isn't all for nothing in the end. Mother didn't need to send you at all. I just need more time."

"**That's** your problem? Things are going too well? Are you kidding? You know, some of us have really tough missions! If you ask me, I think it's yourself you're kidding. I think you're enjoying yourself too much. What's with the hair, for instance? You never leave it down at home—you say it gets in your way. Don't get me wrong, it's pretty that way. But it makes you look like a different person. And don't think I missed the little flutter of your eyes when you talk about this Mowan person. Don't get your heart broken—I'm pretty sure you two don't have a future together written in the stars!"

"That's not true!" Polly insisted. "Mowan's a good friend, and he's cute and all, but…"

"No 'buts' about it. You're smitten! And not just with Mowan, but with the whole thing. You should be grateful Mother didn't send Calliope or Clio. They'd chew you up and spit you out for turning all soft and mushy about your kid and some boy from next-to-nowhere! What about us? What about what we owe each other? What about pear sorbet, for Zeus's sake?"

Polly sank onto the bed. "OK, maybe you're right. It does feel good to get away from everyone and everything and have some adventures of my own. It's been awesome inventing who I want to be here and trying new things. Honestly, Rani, you and I are the serious, studious sisters. Don't you ever get tired of being dutiful and doing what everyone expects of you?"

"A little, I guess," Urania admitted.

"And what if I'm right? What if things have been too easy and won't last unless I make sure Pirra's all set? You're still working on your mission, right? Surely you're not the only one still out there. It's not like all the rest are moping around Mt. Helicon waiting for me to finish and get back. So what if I'm having some fun in the meantime? Isn't that just making the best of things, like I'm supposed to help Pirra do?"

Urania sighed. "You're pretty convincing. I just hope Mother's convinced, too. Be careful, Polly. Don't blow this for us. Finish your mission and go home! Now I'm going to go do the same." As Urania leaned in to hug her sister goodbye, she whispered, "Have fun. We'll talk about this dutiful thing later. Maybe it's time to shake things up a little at home." And the next moment, she was gone.

Polly, Pirra, and Mowan bounced along the road to Alice Springs, laughing and talking about the mural project. They had to shout to be heard over the noisy old Jeep, which added to the hilarity. It made what Polly had to do harder, but she knew if she didn't speak up she'd lose her nerve. At a break in the conversation she announced, "I talked to my parents last night. My dad got called back to work early and they want me to come home."

Pirra turned to Polly in the back seat with alarm in her eyes. "No, Polly, you can't! It's not time for school to start yet. What will I do without you? Who's going to play math games with me?"

Mowan seemed startled, too. "I knew you weren't staying, but I hadn't thought about your leaving, yet. Do you really have to go?"

"Yeah, I do. I have a few more days. I made sure I could do the mural. But they really want to see me and I need to spend some time with my sisters before school starts. I'm really going to miss you two."

The rest of the ride passed quietly. Pirra slumped silently in the front seat. Mowan tried some casual conversation, but gave up and turned on the radio.

There was no time to feel sorry for themselves when they reached the Museum. Lark, in take-charge mode, gathered them and a few other volunteers around like baby chicks and briefed them on plans for the week. Her excitement was catching. Soon the children began to arrive, and they moved into the studio. Each participant would create several original designs, based on traditional Aboriginal symbols, to contribute to the mural. They worked with paint on textured paper. Lark moved around the room, peering over shoulders and encouraging everyone. Polly noticed that she kept returning to look at Pirra's designs.

"This is nice work, Pirra," Lark commented. "Very nice. You're really getting a feel for the sacred geometry ideas we talked about. I can't wait to see these designs larger on the mural. And Mowan," she continued, moving around the table, "I know you like working in three dimensions better, but these are very interesting. I wish you could stay past today."

Polly's efforts were more like diagrams than art, she knew. Her gifts, and those of her sisters, shone more in literature, performing arts, and academics than visual art. During a break she studied Pirra's three designs and was suddenly struck with an idea. *This one would look amazing set into the water-theme wall sculpture in Mowan's studio! And this one seems made to fit on the flat surface in the middle of the large "resting place" piece he just finished. Mowan's sculptures as frames for Pirra's prints? That's perfect! Just what I need!*

The next three days flew by in a combination of creative rush and babysitting chores as the group of artists gradually transformed a boring concrete wall into a swirling dreamtime collage of colorful images and symbols. It was breathtaking, and one of the most rewarding things Polly or Pirra had ever experienced. Passersby stopped to watch and praise the artists, whose confidence and pride grew steadily. Each evening, back at Lark's home, they would pace and chatter, full of the day's energy and sure they'd never be able to sleep, only to fall quickly into deep slumber. By unspoken agreement, they didn't discuss Polly's upcoming departure. When Mowan returned to help with the final touches and take the girls back, all he could do was grin. "This is fantastic. I'm speechless!"

The buzz of conversation on the way home wound down. At first, the silence was a comfortable, contented one. But then Pirra tapped Polly's shoulder from her place in the back of the Jeep. "I **hate** that you have to leave! I just had one of the best experiences of my life with friends I just met but feel like I've know forever, and now you're leaving? That's just not fair! You made this all happen, Polly. And you're the only friend close enough to get to on my own. What am I going to do without you?"

Polly couldn't answer. Tears spilled from her eyes and clogged her throat. She knew just how Pirra felt. Her job was to help Pirra adjust and be happy, and now look at them! They were both miserable! *This is success?* she thought bitterly.

Calm, sensible Mowan tried to lighten the moment. "Come on, you two! You're getting my seat covers soggy. It's not that bad! We've had some great times. Pirra, I won't leave you to waste away all alone. I'll visit and take you places when I can, and I know Kalee wants to get to know you better, too. I'll bet your parents will take you into Alice to keep volunteering, when they see how much you like it. And Polly, you can come back on your next school break, right?"

"I'll try," Polly muttered, knowing it would probably never happen. She knew her job was almost finished, and that Pirra would be fine without her. But thoughts of her sisters and home gave her little comfort. Still, she did look forward to the surprise she had planned when they got back to Pine Creek.

When they arrived, Polly steered the others away from the house and toward Mowan's studio. From her suitcase she pulled two of Pirra's paper designs for the mural, which she'd taken from the Museum.

"Now just look, you two. I thought of something this week. Watch and be amazed!" She crossed the studio and placed Pirra's designs exactly where she had imagined them, with Mowan's pieces. She stood back excitedly. "Do you see what I see? Your styles go together perfectly! Pirra's prints in Mowan's frames. It's genius! You absolutely have to work together. And aside from the art being a perfect match, it will be another reason for you to get together and keep each other entertained and out of trouble. As long as I can go online and see the work you're doing together, I won't miss you so much and I'll know you're both OK. I'll bet you could even sell this stuff! It's as good as work we saw at the Museum. What do you think?"

Pirra looked at Mowan. Mowan looked at Pirra. They both looked at their individual creations, setting each other off as though it was meant to be. Mowan spoke first. "I'd never have thought to put them together like that. I never thought of my pieces as frames. But they do look pretty great together, don't they?"

"They really, really do," Pirra agreed.

"I don't have much time to commit to something new." Mowan sat on a bench, thinking hard. "But this isn't really a new thing, is it? It's just time with my hobby and time with my friend. As long as you don't get your hopes up too much, I'm game to try. It does make a good excuse for us to get together."

"And I've got nothing but time," Pirra observed. "I already decided this week that I want to do more of this kind of art on my own. I suppose once school starts we'll both have less time, but it would be fun to see what we can do until then."

"Yes!" Polly shouted. "And that's good because I already talked to Lark about it and she says, after what she saw this

47

week, she'd like to see some of your combined work. They might want to sell it in the Museum gift shop." Polly's smile was almost smug.

"You did **what**?" demanded Pirra, unsure whether to be angry or thrilled. "That's pretty nervy, considering we hadn't even thought about making art together!"

Mowan's laugh warmed the room. "I've got to say, you're a lot sneakier than you look! Who'd have thought you'd show up and turn everything upside down? We'll really miss you, you little schemer." And he folded them into a group hug.

Polly couldn't bear to say goodbye, so she found another way. When Mr. Morgan left for work the next day he found a small package on the doorstep, addressed to Pirra. In it was a note, explaining that Polly had returned to her grandparents' house to find that her parents had arranged her flight for the next day. She didn't know when she'd be back, but she'd never forget her time there and would keep up with Pirra and Mowan online. Also in the package was a box of business cards, featuring a photo of one of the sculpture-framed prints, for "Moon and Sun Creations: Art from the Outback. Pirra Morgan and Mowan Taylor."

Footnotes

1. Pegasus, famous winged horse ridden by gods and heroes, was entrusted to the Muses after his birth, for his care and training. They came to love him. He would have made a most convenient, if rather conspicuous, mode of transportation for Polly!

2. These monsters have heads and wings like eagles and bodies like lions. Gods and goddesses use them to guard their treasures. Most can fly, but riding them is hazardous. It's thrilling when they soar through the sky, but startling when they turn their sights to dive-bombing someone trying to steal the treasures they protect.

3. The Arrernte people are the indigenous people who lived, and still live, in central Australia.

4. "Greetings" in the Arrernte language
5. "Friend" in the Arrernte language

CHAPTER 4
EUTERPE'S MISSION: LOSING WINGS, FINDING WINGS

Euterpe, Muse of Lyric Poetry and Music, there's a young girl in Canada with real musical promise. But she's been led to believe that her voice is her gift, which is most unfortunate. With your talents for lyric song and flute, your cheerful nature and compassion, you're just the Muse to steer her away from dangerous self-delusion and toward her musical destiny, without crushing her budding artistic spirit.

Prince Albert, Saskatchewan, Canada
"Brava! Brava! Brava!"

Lily soaked up the applause. As usual, her mother and father were on their feet, shouting and clapping loudly. Her toddler sister Hayden hopped up and down, dark curls bouncing, and added her shouts to the clamor. Lily beamed. Her new dress was just right—sparkly and shiny. She'd wrung every drop of feeling out of that old ballad and solidly hit the high note. *But it's getting kind of embarrassing,* she thought as she curtsied and tossed her own straight, dark hair. *Mom and Dad should be more modest when I perform. I don't want the other singers or their parents to feel bad. Maybe I should talk to them.*

She smiled brightly and held her head high, just as her mother had taught her, as she left the stage. She was the last performer in the school program, so Mom caught up with her and folded her into a huge hug almost before she reached the stage door. At ten, Lily was nearly as tall as her mother. But Mom made up in sheer, fluttering energy for her small size.

"Brilliant, Lily! You've never sounded better. Mrs. Edwards was wise to save you for last. After all, who could follow that performance? It would be a shame to make anyone try. Now let's hurry. Your father and Hayden are heading across the street to Jimbo's for a little celebration and then we'll get you home to rest your voice."

Mom chatted on as she steered Lily through the crowd of students, parents, teachers, and relatives. Some greeted Lily. Echoes of "Way to go" and "Nice song, Lily" barely reached her ears over her mother's chirpy voice and the general din. The two moved in a self-contained cloud of excitement, which widened when they entered the old-fashioned diner where Dad was already bragging about her and accepting congratulations from everyone who was anyone in town. Dad was a big man to start with, but his expansive, jovial personality filled the room.

"Hot cocoa all around," he announced grandly, to the sound of more applause. "Here's my little songbird! Lovely, lovely. Soon Prince Albert will be too small to contain your talent."

"Yiwy sing **youd**!" shouted Hayden, and wrapped Lily's knees in a big baby hug.

As they sat in the cozy booth sipping cocoa, Lily sighed contentedly. Lively conversation buzzed around her and the fragrant steam tickled her nose. The tingling energy of performance began to give way to sleepy musings. Tonight had been fun. Nothing felt as good as applause! But she'd sung for school before, and for church, for family holidays, and her parents' dinner parties for town leaders. What made tonight different was that she felt ready now for the upcoming contest. *My first competition!* she thought. *I'm barely old enough to compete. But how often does a chance like this come along?* The popular TV show, *Talented Canada*, was sending scouts to Prince Albert, and this time they were adding a "Talented Young Canada" contest for children ten to fourteen. Child singers, dancers, and musicians were getting their own spin-off show. Mom was sure this was Lily's big chance. The kids' show was a new twist on the TV talent show theme. It would even feature First Nation traditional arts. General auditions were a month away and Lily couldn't wait.

Later, as Mom tucked Lily into bed, she was still raving about Lily's performance. "The song you did tonight is perfect for the audition! Well-known and traditional, but you bring your own style to it. It's a crowd-pleaser."

"I like it. But, Mom, I was wondering. There will be so many singers trying out. You're Cree [1], so I'm half Cree, and there will be less competition for the First Nation segments. Should I practice that Cree lullaby Mrs. Edwards taught us instead?"

"Oh, my, no." Mom waved away the thought. "It's a sweet little song, but so unsophisticated. It wouldn't show off your talent well at all. And you don't need to worry about competition, darling. I'm sure there will be no one else with your gifts and stage presence. We'll let the little Cree children from Pelican Lake have their chance to shine. They don't need to be up against someone like you."

Lily smiled, drifted off to sleep, and dreamed of bowing graciously before millions of TV viewers as she accepted the "Talented Young Canada" winner's crown.

The next Tuesday Mom picked Lily up from school. Hayden cheerfully chanted "Yiwy, Yiwy" from the back seat; Mom was even livelier than usual.

"Wait 'til you see what I found in the paper!" She rescued a section of the *Prince Albert Daily Herald* from Hayden's sticky grasp and thrust it at Lily. "Doesn't it sound perfect? Just the thing to give you a little extra edge in the competition!"

Lily read the offer in the ad section, circled in red:

Talented Young Canada Contestants: Coach for Hire!

Highly experienced performer and winner of dozens of talent competitions ready to guide a promising young artist through the upcoming auditions, with an insider's knowledge and tips on everything from preparation and costumes to on-camera presence and grace in victory! Reasonable fees. Contact sunnymuse@olympus.org.

Lily frowned. Was Mom worried that she wasn't up to the auditions? Did she doubt that Lily could win on her own? *Do I really need extra help?* Before she could ask, Mrs. Lawrence sensed her concern.

"You know, darling, we have every confidence in your talent. But you've never competed before, and I've never done anything like this, either. I know about judged exhibitions for my students at the Arts Center, but they're not the same thing at all. This coach could help us handle details, so nothing gets in the way of letting your voice be heard, so to speak." Mom reached over from the driver's seat and patted Lily's knee. "I've already contacted her and we had a good visit on the phone. She's coming over this evening to meet you and talk about whether we should work together."

Lily caught her mother's excitement. *It does sound perfect! Probably lots of contestants will have voice teachers, but how many will have their own talent show coaches?* She felt important and proud as she imagined being led through the process by a professional. She pictured a woman in a crisp, dark suit, full of authority, shouting, "Make way, make way," as Lily moved toward the stage. She saw herself in a glamorous gown, with her hair upswept and topped by a tiara. By the time they reached home, Lily was as eager as her mother for the doorbell to ring.

When it did ring, Lily was startled. The woman standing before them was young—not more than twenty—and not much taller than Lily herself. A little plump, with chubby pink cheeks, odd violet eyes, and blonde hair pulled back in a frizzy pony tail. She wore a tunic over flowing, wide-legged pants, sandals over socks, and a sparkly headband. Altogether, her appearance was both charmingly artistic and distinctly unprofessional. Lily glanced at Mom, whose big eyes echoed her own surprise. Hayden was uncharacteristically quiet. But the woman, who introduced herself as Sunny, spoke with an exotic accent in a voice that was warm and melodic. By the time they settled in the living room and Mom served tea, they were all enchanted. Hayden climbed onto Sunny's lap to play with her hair.

"You're younger than I imagined," commented Mom, trying her best to be objective and businesslike. "Please tell us about your experience with talent shows. Lily's father, Mr. Lawrence, will join us soon. He was kept late at a City Council meeting, but he said to go ahead without him."

Sunny (usually known as Euterpe) impressed them with her confidence and cheerfulness, as she described singing and playing instruments with her sisters at countless banquets and competitions. She confided, with pride, that while many musicians had challenged the sisters, they had never defeated them. Lily's father arrived in time to hear this encouraging claim and fell happily under Sunny's spell as well. She assured them that she and her family ensemble were well known in Greece, where she grew up, and even beyond. By the end of the conversation, Lily and her parents were sold. Dad pulled out his checkbook.

"You'll need a retainer, of course. Money is no object when it comes to supporting our little rising star. When can you begin working with Lily?"

"Let's start right away. How's tomorrow after school?"

OK, thought Euterpe as she drove back to the Prince Albert Inn, where she'd booked a room. *That's settled. Now what? I need to hear her sing to be sure her voice is really bad, not just untrained. She's so eager, and her parents are so sure of her talent. I'll have to be careful or I'll upset her and anger them. Daddy's clearly a bigwig around here and they aren't used to being questioned, let alone contradicted. But then what? How do I figure out what her real musical gift is?* Sunny sighed, wishing she were back on Mount Helicon with her sisters. Even their squabbling seemed comfortable and familiar, and didn't carry all this responsibility. *Well, Mother thought I was right for this job, so I guess I'll just take it one step at a time.*

When Sunny arrived the next afternoon, she surprised Lily and Mom by announcing that she had reserved a practice room at the Diefenbaker Theater, where the auditions would take place. "We might as well start right out getting a feel for the site," she explained.

"But Hayden's sleeping," Mom protested. "I don't want to wake her."

"That's OK, Mrs. Lawrence, as long as you're comfortable with my taking Lily. It'll give us a chance to get to know each other."

Mom agreed, and out the door they went. They climbed into Sunny's car.

"Should I sing for you while we drive?" Lily offered.

"Sure." Sunny turned on the radio to find a song for Lily to sing along with.

"I don't need that. I can sing alone. My mom thinks I have perfect pitch." Lily launched into the ballad she had sung in the school concert, with great earnestness and… well… volume.

Oh, dear, thought Sunny. *Mother was right. She has a decent sense of pitch, but that harsh tone! And has no one taught this girl anything about dynamics and phrasing? No doubt about it, I'll be doing her a favor by making sure she doesn't humiliate herself in competition.*

Lily finished the song and looked at Sunny, expecting the praise she was used to. Sunny hesitated.

"Well, Lily, thank you for your song." Sunny chose her words carefully. "I can tell you really love singing. You sing with such enthusiasm! We can build on that, I think."

"Oh… You're welcome. Did you like it? When can I hear you sing?"

"Let's get to the Theatre. We can sing something together then."

"OK. I'll bet you're really good."

"So I've been told. We'll see."

They found the practice room easily. Lily had been to the Theatre for performances many times, but she'd never seen this "behind the scenes" part of the building. It thrilled her to walk past practice rooms, storage areas for scenery and props, and a couple of dressing rooms. *Maybe I'll get a dressing room of my own when I win,* she thought to herself.

The tiny practice room was uncluttered, with bare walls, a piano, piano bench, music stand, and chair. Sunny sat on the bench and motioned Lily to the chair.

"Let's try the ballad you sang in the car as a duet. Just start singing. I'll figure out some harmony." Lily launched into the song. Soon Sunny's voice began to soar above Lily's, so achingly sweet and lovely that Lily was stunned into silence.

"Why did you stop?" asked Sunny.

"Because... because... I **never** heard anyone sing like that in my whole life! How did you do that?"

"I guess it's just a gift, though my sisters and I do practice a lot."

"Do all of your sisters sing like that?"

"I suppose so. Differently, of course, and some are better instrumentalists than vocalists, but we're all pretty good. I did tell you we'd never lost a competition." Accustomed as she was to praise, Sunny blushed at Lily's open-mouthed awe. "Want to try it again?"

"Yes! This time I'm ready, so I'll keep going."

They sang the song through but Lily tapered off at the end.

"I always thought I was a good singer, but I'm not nearly as good as you."

Be careful, thought Sunny. *She's already starting to question herself. She needs time to get used to the idea that she's not as good as she's always been told.*

"Let's try a different song," Sunny suggested. "And you should sing alone. After all, I won't be singing with you at the audition."

"I'm glad! They'd never even listen to me! Do you think there will be kids in the competition as good as you?"

"Remember, Lily, I'm older than you. I've had lots more time to practice and develop my talent. What other song would you like to sing for me?"

"There's this one I like. My teacher taught it to our class. It's a lullaby that the Native people sing. My mother's Cree, so

I asked her if I should sing it and compete with the First Nation kids, but she said no. She doesn't think it's fancy enough for my voice," Lily explained. "I don't think she likes Cree music much."

"Why do you say that?" asked Sunny.

"I don't know. She never listens to it. She never talks about being Cree. Mom grew up in Leoville, but she never goes there. I've never been there, even though we have relatives there. I think she's sort of embarrassed about it."

"I wonder why. Hmm… Oh well, sing me that lullaby."

Lily sang, more gently than before. *Her tone quality is still wretched,* thought Sunny, *but she's treating this song like music. She seems to understand what a lullaby is. She's even swaying to the rhythm. Maybe there's a musician in there after all.*

When she finished, Sunny risked some cautious praise. "Good! You sang that song like it speaks to you—to your heart. Let me think about that. We have time to decide on the song. Let's finish up with a walk through the building, so you start to get comfortable with the surroundings. Then I'll take you home."

At the Lawrence's door, Lily begged Sunny to come in. "My family has to hear you sing! Please sing for them!"

Dad overheard and chimed in. "Yes, Sunny, won't you grace us with a song? We'd love to hear the voice of the coach we've entrusted our baby to."

Sunny thought fast. *I suppose they'll insist on hearing me eventually. But how will they take it? Will they get upset at the contrast? Do they have musical ears at all? How could they, and still pump Lily up so about her voice? But maybe they need to hear the difference to begin to open up to other possibilities for Lily. I guess it might as well be now.*

"I've got just a minute for a song. Shall we sing the duet, Lily?"

"No, I want them to just hear you," Lily answered, lowering her eyes.

Sunny's song seemed to float in the air long after she left the house. Aside from subdued good-byes, no one spoke of it until Hayden announced, with great seriousness, "Sunny sing pwitty." They all nodded over their dinner plates.

Lily was quiet the next day. She asked her parents not to make such a fuss at her performances, and while she said it was because she didn't want the other singers to feel bad, truthfully, it was as much about a small knot of doubt in her stomach.

"That's so thoughtful of you, Lily," Mom replied, "but we can't help ourselves when you sing so beautifully! I suppose we can try if you're sure that's what you want. Are you feeling well? You're not nervous, are you?"

"Maybe a little. I've never competed before, and I never heard anyone sing like Sunny. What if there are kids at the audition that sound like her?"

Dad protested. "Nonsense, sweetheart. Sunny's had lots more time to practice. The way you sound now, I'm sure you'll be just as good when you're her age. I asked around City Hall, and everyone says yours was the best song in the school program. You'll just have to face it, Lily. Fair to the others or not, you have a gift. You can't 'hide your light under a bushel.' Don't let a little competition scare you."

"I guess you're right, Daddy," Lily agreed, her confidence mostly restored.

Twice more in the coming days, Lily and Sunny met at the Theatre. Sunny, unsure of how to proceed, stalled for time by focusing on logistics of the competition. They reviewed the process step by step. They talked about what Lily might wear and how she should present herself. On Friday, Mrs. Lawrence came with Lily.

"Lily tells me you've been walking through details of the competition. How is her song coming along? We are sticking with the ballad, right? People always love to hear a song they know. May I hear it now?"

"Well," Sunny mumbled, "we have been concentrating on the process so far. There's still plenty of time to make final decisions and polish the actual song...." Her voice faded, revealing indecision.

"That's all well and good, but I'd love to hear the song

now, and your thoughts about showing it off to best advantage."

Mrs. Lawrence was adamant, so Sunny sat down at the piano and played while Lily sang. *Oh dear,* Sunny thought, *she sounds screechier than ever! And now I have to finesse both her and her mom. What can I say? How can they both be so sincere and so oblivious?*

"Ah, that's our girl! What do you think, Sunny? Will she stun the judges?"

"She sings her heart out, that's for sure." Sunny struggled for words, as an idea began to form in her mind. "We need to work on phrasing and dynamics. I have an idea for doing that. We'll start on it Monday."

"We trust your judgment, Sunny. I'm sure you'll know just how to put the finishing touches on her performance. Those judges will be so dazzled they'll need sunglasses!" Mrs. Lawrence seemed satisfied that they were, again, on track. Mother and daughter left happy; Sunny stayed behind.

OK, time to face facts. I do know how to help with techniques, but that won't make her a singer. She needs to know that, and soon. Mighty Olympus! I never could stand to hurt anyone's feelings. What made Mother think I could do this? I need some sister help, and I know which one. Bossy, pushy Calliope isn't always my favorite, but I think she's just what this situation needs. Sunny tapped out the code on her fingers. In an instant Calliope appeared, windblown and out of breath.

"This had better be important!" Calliope blustered. "I'm spending so much time coaching the rest of you through your missions that I hardly have time for my own!"

"Of course you are," Sunny responded dryly. "Of course it's important, or I wouldn't have called you. I'm in a fix, and I think this tricky situation needs a bit of your... shall we say... directness. Here's the story...."

Bringing Calliope up to speed took a while, as Calli kept interrupting.

"You're calling yourself **Sunny**? Are you kidding? Where did **that** come from? Though I must admit it suits your annoyingly cheerful personality."

"I've always wanted to be called Sunny! You know I tried at home and you all just laughed at me. But how many 'Euterpes' are there in Canada? I'm trying not to blow my cover. Anyway, that's beside the point...."

"And what's wrong with these people? Don't they have ears? No doubt caught up in that 'self-esteem' nonsense mortals are so keen on, as though they're doing their little darlings a favor by convincing them that every puny, pathetic effort amounts to genius!"

When Sunny finally finished telling the tale, Calliope sat back, looked her straight in the eyes, and stated, with annoyance, "Isn't it obvious? You just have to **tell** her! Honestly! I'm not as heartless as you all seem to think, but there's truth to the saying that sometimes 'you've got to be cruel to be kind.' The contest is only three weeks away! Her deluded parents complicate things, for sure. But this coaching thing you've got going is a good plan. You just need to give them a dose of reality! If Mother says she has musical promise, then finding her real instrument will soften the blow. But you can't keep stringing them along. If you don't have the guts, I can do it for you—maybe as a consulting expert or something—but it has to be quick. I have my own work to do."

"No!" Calli would smash Lily and infuriate her parents for sure, with her lack of tact. "You're right, but I have to do it. I just need a little more time to figure out what her real gift is."

"Well, get moving! Time's running out. And remember, you only get one more sister bail-out! Call if you need me." Calliope disappeared.

The next week Sunny was still trying to find the courage to tell Lily and her parents the hard truth. But she had, if not a real plan, at least some ideas. Sunny's flute, her signature instrument, was perfect for demonstrating dynamics and phrasing skills, so she brought it along to the Theatre. Also, Sunny had started checking out the competition by listening in on other contestants in the Theatre's practice rooms. *Some of the singers are quite good. Maybe if Lily hears them...* So Sunny scheduled their next practice at the same time that two talented young singers had reserved rooms.

On the way in, Sunny led Lily past those practice rooms. While insulation muffled the sound some, they could hear both singers—a boy about Lily's age and a girl a little older—quite clearly. Sunny watched Lily's face for reactions. Lily's steps slowed. *Does that frown mean she's concerned?* In their own practice room, Sunny observed casually, "Those kids we passed sounded pretty good, didn't they?"

Lily nodded silently, her brow wrinkling.

OK, this is it, Sunny thought. *Handle this right and maybe she'll start to get it. Give her some time to think while you do what you promised to do.*

"I said we'd work on dynamics and phrasing today. I brought my flute because it's good for showing those things. I'm going to play the ballad for you. Listen closely. Notice when I breathe and how I change the volume and pace to fit the changing emotions in the melody. Ready?"

Lily nodded.

As Sunny played, Lily's eyes widened. By the end of the first verse, they were filled with tears.

"Lily, what's wrong?"

"Nothing." Lily's voice quivered. "It's just so beautiful! It almost hurts to listen. I've sung that song a hundred times and I never knew it could be so beautiful."

The two sat without speaking for a long moment. Finally, Lily broke the silence.

"Sunny, could we work on the other song? The lullaby? I don't think I could sing that one after hearing you play it. It just seems like it belongs to your flute. It wouldn't feel right. I think I can convince Mom I like the other song better, especially if you help. I can usually get them to do what I want when I try."

"Sure. Let's try it. A real musician couldn't ever give her best performance with music that doesn't feel right."

What's this? Sunny wondered. *She's obviously moved by the flute. Could that be the true musician in her? Is this Mother's little joke? Could it be that obvious, and I've been missing it all along? Time to find out.*

"Lily, let me ask you something. You know the way you felt when I played the flute just now. Is that how you feel when you sing?"

Lily frowned again. "It's different. When I sing, I get excited." She paused and shifted in her chair. "I love being on the stage. I love when people clap. I love how proud Mom and Daddy get, and being in the spotlight. But listening to the flute made me feel sort of peaceful and achy and fluttery, all at the same time."

Sunny concentrated on Lily's words and intense expression. *I think we're onto something here.* She closed her eyes tightly while she summoned her courage and formed the right words.

"Then tell me this—You love the praise people give you when you sing. What do they say?"

Lily blinked at her. "What do you mean, what do they say?"

"What actual words do they use? Not your parents, but others. I want you to think carefully about what other people say when they praise you."

Lily's eyes focused on the wall as she concentrated, trying to recall details from what always felt like the general flurry of post-performance.

"I never paid much attention to the actual words. Um, I think they say stuff like 'You sing with such feeling,' or 'I could hear you all the way in the back row,' or just 'Good job!'"

Lily's eyes widened again. She fixed a look on Sunny that was first questioning, then pleading. "But those words... They don't say... Shouldn't they say...? Do you mean... Does that mean I'm really not such a good singer after all?"

"I think it means that we need to think more about your music. I know there's a real musician in you. I'm just not sure singing is the right choice."

"But why would everyone say... Why would they all make such a fuss and ask me to sing? Why would my parents tell me how good I am?" Sunny saw the beginnings of alarm and then tears in Lily's eyes.

"People want to encourage you, and maybe please your parents. And your parents? Well, they're not musicians themselves, are they? They're important people in town, who are used to being right and who love you and think everything you do is perfect...."

"No! You're wrong," Lily erupted. "You're just being mean! You're jealous because I'm such a good singer and you don't want anyone else to be as good as you! I don't want to talk to you anymore. I want to go home!" Lily ran out of the room, down the hall, and out the door, sobbing. Sunny followed, almost equally upset.

I've done it now! So much for "cruel to be kind." I've squashed her spirit for sure, and her mom and dad will be beyond furious!

Sunny ran for the car and caught up with Lily, who shivered visibly in the cold, a block down the street.

"Please, Lily, get in the car. I know you're upset, but at least let me drive you home so I know you're safe. We can talk about this. I really do want to help."

Lily slowed and finally stopped. "I'll get in the car, but only because I need a ride home. I don't want to talk to you. I don't want to talk to anybody. **No talking**!"

"OK, OK. No talking. I'll take you home."

The short ride home was the most uncomfortable, unhappy ten minutes Sunny could remember [2]. Lily jumped from the car and ran inside, leaving Sunny to imagine the scene that must be playing out in the house.

Inside, Mom was beside herself. She flitted between clutching her teary daughter and pacing the living room, emitting alternating waves of pity and fury from her tiny frame.

"Sunny said **what**? How could she? Who does she think she is, upsetting my baby like this?" She stopped pacing and slammed her fist on the sofa back. "Why, that vain little traitor! I'll bet she's jealous. That's it! Miss 'never lost a competition' can't stand the thought of a talent superior to her own! I'll tell your father! I'll have him stop payment on her check! I'll have the City Council throw her out of town! And I'll start by calling her and giving her a piece of my mind!"

Mom's intensity frightened Lily. Lily was angry, too, but she had stopped sobbing and started thinking. Events of the past week and bits of memories from past events swirled in her head. *It isn't all Sunny's fault,* she thought. She was starting to realize, deep down, that there was more to the story, even if she wasn't prepared to accept it yet. Right now, she needed to calm her mother down—almost as though she were the parent, trying to protect Mom from her own hurt feelings.

"It's OK, Mom, really. I'm OK. Don't call Sunny. She may be wrong, but I don't think she meant to be mean. Maybe we shouldn't get so upset. You don't want to wake up Hayden."

Luckily, the role reversal wasn't lost on Mom. She took a deep breath. "You're right. Bless your sweet heart; at the very least I need to collect myself. We will hold Sunny accountable, but we'll do it with grace and dignity. That's how we Lawrences do things."

That evening, while Lily did homework in her room, her parents talked in the kitchen. They tried to be quiet, but they were simply not quiet people. The conversation kept exploding into angry crescendos and then, as one parent tried to calm the other, settling back to a quieter buzz. Lily didn't know what she wanted to happen. She was confused and miserable, but she wasn't sure whom to be mad at.

Sunny, wandering beside the snow-covered river deep in thought, was also confused and miserable. *What have I done? What could I have done? What should I do now? I have to face the Lawrences, even if all I can hope for is damage control. But I can't fail in my mission! I can't be the one to let everyone down. Poor Lily! I thought we'd made a breakthrough. I can even guess her real talent, after the way she reacted to my flute. But how can I get her to trust me again, even if her parents would let me near her? I'll bet no one has been this angry with me since Marsyas [3]. I hate to admit it, but I think I need Calli again.*

She tapped out the code. Calliope joined her on the path and pulled her into the Band Stand.

"Well, here I am again. It's freezing out here! Let's at least get out of the wind. So did you break the news to her? How'd she take it?"

At least Calli didn't seem cranky about the interruption. Sunny felt bad enough without having to deal with Calli's temperament.

"I did tell her. And I think I know what her instrument is.

64

But she's so upset that I'm not sure I'll ever get to tell her that part! It was too much of a shock. She doesn't believe me and now she hates me. And I'd guess, by now, her parents want my head in a sack [4]. Oh, Calli, I've messed up. What can I do?"

"Relax. I have a plan. I figured you'd have trouble being straight with her, so I've been thinking about how to salvage the mission. After all, I'm not about to give up pear sorbet without a fight!" Calli let out a deep, dramatic sigh. "What would you all do without me?"

In spite of Calli's superior attitude, Sunny was open to anything. "What's the plan?"

"Here's what I'm thinking. Your coaching ad was smart. We can build on that. If someone would offer to coach contestants through the competition, why wouldn't someone else offer to prepare them by giving them a taste of the judging process?" Calli's voice rose in pitch as she warmed to the cleverness of her own plan. "You've seen the TV talent shows that are all the rage among mortals, with their panels of famous judges. Why not stage a practice competition with a judge who'll tell the cold, hard truth? Someone who's objective, impartial and, well, not **you**? Someone who's here and then gone, so there's no one to catch the fallout. Someone like me!"

"I don't know, Calli. You're not exactly tactful, and Lily's really fragile right now. She's so miserable! Do you suppose this is how the Sirens felt when they lost their wings [5]? As things stand now, I'm not sure Lily would even go to a practice judging, and if she did it might be too hard on her. What if she gave up music altogether?"

"Mother said she has real potential, right? Real musicians don't give up. And tact is overrated. Haven't you seen Simon, the brutally honest judge on TV talent shows? People love him! Don't worry about a thing. Just leave it to me!"

Calliope vanished.

"**No**, wait! Calli, come back! You can't just take over my mission! **Wait!**" But Calli was gone.

Oh, no! From bad to worse! Why did I ever ask Calli for help? I should have known she'd take over. She'll ruin things for Lily, for me, and for all of us! Like it or not, I have to get to the Lawrences before she does.

By the time she reached her car, Sunny realized that it was too late in the evening to talk to Lily and her family. It would have to wait until morning, and then Lily would be in school. *Do I dare confront Mrs. Lawrence alone?* Angry as Lily was at her, Sunny knew that it was nothing compared to what she'd face from Mrs. Lawrence! *I have no choice. I'll go first thing in the morning.*

Sunny rang the Lawrences' doorbell at 8:30 AM, but got no answer. She waited in the car, drumming on the steering wheel and chewing her fingernails. When Mrs. Lawrence returned home with Hayden about 11:00, Sunny met her at the door.

Mrs. Lawrence lit into her instantly. "What are you doing here? Don't you think you've done enough damage? What were you thinking, telling Lily that she wasn't a singer? I'd thought better of you, but your cruelty is inexcusable. You need to leave now and never come back!"

"Please, Mrs. Lawrence," Sunny begged. "Just give me a minute to explain. I know you and Lily are hurt and angry, but I'm really just trying to help and I want to be sure Lily isn't hurt even more by something you might hear about soon...."

"Ah, now I understand," Mrs. Lawrence interrupted. "I'll bet you're talking about this!" She pulled another newspaper ad from her large handbag. "Mr. Lawrence and I were beside ourselves trying to figure out how to restore Lily's confidence. But this is just the thing! A fair and impartial practice judge will hear Lily and give her the praise she deserves, and she'll realize that you were just jealous! Of course, you wouldn't want that to happen because it will expose you as the mean-spirited fraud you are! Well, too bad for you! Lily **will** attend this event. She'll sing her heart out and we'll all be back on course—all but you, that is. Now leave us alone!" She carried Hayden into the house and slammed the door.

Sunny trudged back to her car. *I can't believe what a mess this is! We'll never have pear sorbet again, and it'll be as much my fault as it is Calli's, for asking for her help.* For a second, she let herself hope that the ad was a coincidence—

that someone else really was offering to be a "practice judge" and that it wasn't Calli's work at all. But that was ridiculous. Of course, it was Calli. *The others will never forgive me. Worse than that, Lily will never forgive me. I can't let that happen!*

Sunny hadn't seen the ad itself, so she went in search of a newspaper. Sure enough, there it was. It was big and surrounded by stars sprouting like flowers from a leafy border. The ornate design and self-important wording had "Calliope" written all over them. The event was scheduled for 6:30 PM on Saturday *(That's tomorrow!)* at the Theatre. Sunny's emotions swung wildly, from hope to discouragement to anger to determination and around again. But right now she needed the energy of anger. She tapped out the code to call Calli to her. No response. She tried again. Nothing. Was Calli ignoring her, or was the signal not getting through because of Mother's rule about two assists per mission? Either way, Calli was not answering. Sunny pounded the steering wheel and shouted some very ungoddessly curses at her absent sister before remembering Mother's warning about conflict during the missions. *And where **is** Mother in all of this? Does she know what Calli's doing? Will she allow it? Am I failing so miserably that she's actually letting Calli take over? Well, if this mission is going to fail, cost us all our pear sorbet forever, and make my sisters hate me, I have to salvage something from it! I have to at least soften the blow for Lily! Breathe and think, breathe and think....*

Slightly calmer, Sunny considered her options. Could she stop the event from happening? Maybe she could talk to the Theatre manager or the *Talented Canada* people and discredit Calliope. *No,* she reminded herself. *That will backfire if they start looking into my role here. To have a chance of making anything good out of this, I have to protect my cover.* Could she keep Lily from showing up? *How? The Lawrences won't let me near Lily, let alone listen to anything I might say. And Mother was clear about "ordinary interaction" only, so that rules out any hocus-pocus.* She could try to catch Calliope before the event and talk her out of it. *But when has Calliope ever let anyone talk her out of anything? She's always so sure she's right and knows better.* In the end, all Sunny could think to do was to be there, at the judging, to make whatever difference she could in what promised to be a disaster for Lily and for her mission.

Saturday evening was snowy and windy. Sunny arrived early, hoping to catch Calliope and at least try to talk some sense into her. But the door to the auditorium was locked, and a uniformed guard announced that the only people allowed inside were the judge and one contestant, with up to two family members, at a time. Sunny's lame appeal that she was coaching a contestant—a fact the Lawrences would dispute when they arrived, anyway—fell on deaf ears. If she obeyed the "normal interaction" rule, which she knew she had to, she was stuck outside to imagine the disaster and hope for some unlikely turn of luck. She sat down in the hallway and pulled out her flute. She could, at least, comfort herself with music.

Sunny saw Lily and her parents enter the Theatre through the side door and move into the waiting space in the auditorium wings. She crept along behind them and watched for an opportunity to sneak inside. When a custodian left the backstage area, carrying a mop and pushing a bucket, Sunny ducked behind a display case and caught the door before it latched. *Whew! I'm in. Now I can at least listen without being seen.*

Calliope sat at a small table on the far side of the stage, looking crisp and official in a tailored pantsuit. A young dancer was finishing his tap routine. Sunny watched Calli lean back in her chair, smirking. As the boy concluded his rather ragged performance, Calli sighed. "Well, Jerome, I have to say that the only thing more unfortunate than your choice of music is your clumsiness! With the competition only two weeks away, I can't imagine you'll achieve anything like real dancing in time. In fact, I suggest you accept that performing is simply not in your future and stick to the school dance floor, where you may succeed in impressing a few uncultured young ladies. Next!"

Sunny gasped and watched poor, deflated Jerome scurry off the stage with his head down.

Next up was a Cree boy, a little older than Lily. He mounted the stage with confidence and sang a traditional war song. His strong, clear voice, while untrained, was pleasing and expressive. Sunny wondered what Calli would find to fault in him. When he finished, he held his head high and looked directly at Calliope. "Raymond, you have a lot to learn about using your voice to best effect, and I don't know that you're ready for competition. But there's no denying you have talent. Get a good vocal coach and keep practicing." Sunny had to admit that, while she hated this whole situation and dreaded what was coming, Calli was judging honestly and fairly.

Raymond left the auditorium. The waiting room door opened and Sunny watched Lily move toward the stage, followed closely by Mr. and Mrs. Lawrence. Sunny's heart sank. While Lily looked charming in a dark green dress and stylish boots, her hesitant steps and drooping posture told Sunny that she was nervous. For a moment, Sunny wondered if it might have been better to let her hold onto her fantasy of singing stardom as long as she could. But, of course, that couldn't have lasted and was bound to end badly. Sunny couldn't stand to watch the next few minutes, but she couldn't look away, either.

Calli called Lily onto the stage. "Lily Lawrence. I've heard of you. Come up and begin when you're ready."

Lily climbed the stairs, as her parents whispered encouragement. She nodded at the pianist, who surprised Sunny by playing a simple introduction to the Cree lullaby. *What do you know?* Sunny thought. *She can get her parents to do what she wants. At least she's going with a song that means something to her.* Sunny crossed her fingers tightly, in a gesture she'd seen mortals use "for luck."

Nerves and the upset of recent days did nothing to improve Lily's performance. She botched the pitch and couldn't deliver the sensitivity Sunny had heard in the song before. Sunny cringed, and while broad grins and nods from her parents continued throughout the song, Lily's stiffness and pained expression signaled that she knew the truth.

Calliope hesitated briefly before launching into her Simon impersonation. Sunny caught her breath, hoping for... what? But the moment passed, and Calli asked loudly, "Did someone let a screech owl in here? Such a sweet old song, but I could hardly tell what it was for the caterwauling. Do you really think you're a singer, dear? I'm afraid you've been misinformed. Perhaps you should try the cello. Next!"

After a moment of stunned silence, several things happened at once. Mrs. Lawrence charged the stage stairs with murder in her eyes, shrieking, followed closely by a no-longer-jovial Mr. Lawrence. Sunny almost feared for Calliope, but knew that her sister would come out of the encounter unharmed and disappear completely. While Lily's parents let loose on Calliope, Lily slunk off and ran from the auditorium. Sunny followed.

Lily stumbled on, blinded by tears. Near the end of the hallway she sank to the floor and sobbed, her head in her hands. She didn't see Sunny come up behind her and sit a few feet away. For once, Sunny knew exactly what to do. Wanting only to ease Lily's pain, she pulled out her flute and began to play a quiet, mournful melody. Lily didn't seem to hear at first, but gradually her sobbing slowed and she looked up. Sunny kept playing. Music, not words, would touch Lily at this moment. Lily started to get up, but changed her mind. The short, sad song gave way to a livelier folk tune. It wasn't until Lily managed a small smile that Sunny risked moving from music to words.

"I'm so sorry, Lily. I know you're hurting and I know you're mad at me. But I told you I believed that you're a musician, and I meant it. I knew that for sure when you responded to my flute the way you did. I'm going to leave, since I know our time working together is over. But I want to give you something."

She handed Lily her flute.

"You may not be ready to try this for a while. But I know the musician in you won't let you give up, and I'm sure this is the right instrument for you. Maybe the next time TV scouts come to Prince Albert, you'll be ready to wow the judges and to know in your heart, for sure, that you earned their praise."

Lily accepted the gift with tear-filled eyes and a nod, just as Mr. and Mrs. Lawrence entered the hallway looking for her. Still gulping an occasional sob, Lily turned to Sunny. "You'd better go. My parents are in no mood..." She actually giggled a little. "I wouldn't want to be that judge! But, Sunny, I think I understand. Maybe they will too, after a while. Thanks."

Sunny nodded, stood, and trotted out the exit door at the end of the hall. *I may be a coward,* she told herself, *but I think my work here is done. And even immortals aren't eager to take on suicide missions, though murder might be in order next time I see Calli….*

Six months later, riding home from a weekend on the Pelican Lake First Nation Reserve near Leoville, Lily bubbled with excitement.

"This has been the best day ever! Mrs. Chamakese says she can't believe I've learned so much on the flute so fast! She says I have a natural talent for traditional music! It feels so good to play. It's different from singing, you know? When I sang it was all about me and applause. When I play the flute, it's not about me at all." Lily paused. "I don't know how to describe it, but I sort of get lost in the music, like only the song matters. Mrs. Chamakese is a really good teacher."

"That's what they tell us. Nothing but the best for our baby," Dad replied, shaking his head "but who would have thought…."

"Mom, thanks for introducing me to Auntie Ronnie. The Powwow was awesome. She said maybe next year I can play for it! Do you think I could? Could we get a traditional costume for me? Please, Mom?"

"Why not, if it makes you happy? It was good to see Ronnie and the others after such a long time. I won't mind these trips at all. It all seems so much more interesting than when I lived there."

"Listen to the new song I learned today!" Lily's flute began a lilting, lively melody. It seemed to fill the car with light. After the second verse, a small, sweet voice joined in the chorus with dreamy nonsense syllables. Lily played through her surprise while two amazed parents listened from the front seat. As the music faded away, Lily smiled and spoke for them all. "Hayden sings pretty!"

Footnotes

1. The Pelican Lake First Nation Cree community lives on and around a settlement on Chitek Lake in Saskatchewan, with headquarters in Leoville.

2. And that's saying something, since Muses are immortal and her life had already been very long!

3. As the story goes, the satyr Marsyas found a flute that had been Athena's. He made such wondrous music with it that he challenged Apollo to a musical contest. The Muses were chosen as judges. Apollo played his lyre against Marsyas's flute. The first round was a tie, which angered Apollo. He insisted that, in the second round, the musicians play their instruments upside down! Marsyas was, of course, unable to play his flute that way and the Muses declared Apollo the winner. Marsyas was enraged by Apollo's trickery and the Muses' complicity.

4. Mortals would probably say "head on a platter," in grim reference to the Biblical story about John the Baptist's execution. This reference is to the Gorgon Medusa's severed head, kept in a bag to protect the unsuspecting from being turned to stone by its glance. This story is no less grisly, but more familiar to Euterpe.

5. Hera, queen of the gods, persuaded the Sirens to challenge the Muses to a singing contest. As beautifully as the Sirens sang, they couldn't match the Muses, so they lost the competition. As punishment for their vanity, the Muses took their wings and used the feathers to make decorations for their hair. The Sirens were banished to islands in the Mediterranean Sea, where they used their songs to lure sailors to their death on the rocky shores. To this day, people in the Greek islands use the expression "losing your wings" to describe how it feels when you find out you're not as good at something as you believed you were.

CHAPTER 5
ERATO'S MISSION: LOVE POEMS

Erato, as Muse of Romantic Poetry, you have the gift of inspiring both love and literature. I've chosen for you a young fellow in Italy who fancies himself quite a ladies' man. He has potential as a poet, but can't seem to focus his attentions on a single young lady long enough to develop either his passion or his poetry beyond the mundane and superficial. It's up to you to help him grow into his gifts.

Florence, Italy

Enzo sighed as he leaned back at his school desk, long legs stretched out before him, and gazed at the back of Jordan's head. Her dark curls swirled in lovely chaos. He wondered how, just days ago, he could have thought Gemma was the girl for him. Gemma was smart, of course, and Enzo liked smart girls. But she didn't have shiny, loopy hair that made you want to run your fingers through it. He was already composing a poem in his mind—something about raven locks and flying flocks, perhaps, and imagining how pleased she would be to receive it. He had to think fast when Signora del Russo called his name. "Master Moretti, please answer question #4 for us."

After class Enzo tried to catch Jordan, but she had rushed out ahead of him and disappeared in the crowd. No matter. He'd wait until he could hand her his poem. He caught up with Gina, his neighbor and best friend, for the short walk home. Enzo had known Gina since they were toddlers, and he was as comfortable with her as he was with his annoying, but amusing, little brother. As they walked, Enzo suddenly realized Gina was talking to him.

"Enzo, did you hear me? Are you trying out for football or not? Oh, Enzo, I know that look. Who is it this time? Don't tell me you're tired of Gemma already?" This was a familiar conversation. Gina couldn't even guess how many times in the last couple of years Enzo had wandered home in a daze, starry-eyed over a new crush.

"Have you ever really looked at Jordan's hair?" Enzo replied. "Does she do something to make it curl like that, or was she born that way? It looks so soft and shiny. What rhymes with "shiny?" But he wasn't really looking for answers.

Gina sighed. He was worse about girls than any of her girlfriends was about boys. But in Enzo's case, it wasn't just the most popular or good-looking ones—the ones you'd want to be "seen with." Enzo really liked girls and was often drawn to people others overlooked.

"Oh, Enzo, not again! Jordan. Gemma. Before that, Tira and Isabella." She ticked them off on her fingers. "And that's just this term! At this rate, you'll set a record for falling in love more than any fourteen-year-old in history!"

To be honest, Gina actually liked Enzo's ability to appreciate things in people that others missed. Most of their classmates thought Tira was odd, but Enzo liked how sweet she was with her puppy. Isabella was rather large, but she made him laugh, and he'd doted on her for weeks. Aside from assuming girls would welcome his attention and treasure his poems, he didn't act conceited. And he was never mean to last week's crush; he simply fell just as totally and hopelessly for the new one, and moved on. Gina shook her head.

"You'll get yourself in trouble yet," she warned, slapping Enzo's shoulder lightly. Enzo hardly noticed, lost as he was in romantic reverie. It was a wonder his fickle attentions didn't get him into more trouble. Some of the girls laughed it off, or even laughed at him behind his back. A few got angry. Some nursed broken hearts and clung to his silly poems as if they were Shakespearean sonnets. But no one seemed to hold a grudge. It was, in a strange way, a badge of honor in their school to have Enzo write you a love poem. The girls' reactions never seemed to faze Enzo. He took it as a matter of course that the past was past, and the current object of his affections was the love of his life... so far.

"You're hopeless!" Gina said, wondering briefly, as she had before, why Enzo never wrote silly poems for her. She dismissed the thought. She didn't want to be another has-been in Enzo's parade of loves. Better to be his friend, the person he talks to, and who keeps his feet somewhere near the ground. *Still, what do those girls have that I don't?*

When she tuned back in, Enzo was chatting pleasantly about football tryouts. This is how it was with them, easy and comfortable. Enzo waved absentmindedly when they reached Gina's villetta. She shook her head and watched him lope across the street and in his door.

That Saturday Enzo eagerly approached Jordan on the way into class and handed her a folded sheet of paper. "This is for you," he said, and hurried to his desk.

Could this be what it looks like, Jordan wondered? She slid into her desk in front of him and flashed him a smile just as Signora del Russo called the class to order. Jordan unfolded the paper to see Enzo's blocky handwriting. She read,

Jordan of the raven locks,
Swirling 'round like flying flocks
Of graceful birds, I wish that I
Could touch those curls and I would fly
With joy into the evening sky.

Well, what do you know? Enzo liked her! She was pleased. Besides being legendary (and somewhat laughable) for his fickle heart and corny poems, he was nice-looking—tall and lanky, with blue eyes and wavy, dark hair—and quite sweet. Maybe he'd ask her to the spring dance.

Enzo made arrangements to walk Jordan home from school on Monday, as he already had plans that afternoon. He'd convinced Gina to check out a new student club with him. The club hadn't appeared on the term's advance list of after-school offerings. But if he'd heard correctly, it was a poetry-writing group, led by a student from a nearby secondary school who was already a published poet, even though she was only a year ahead of Enzo. *That's for me,* Enzo thought. Of course, he had a head start, having already written dozens of poems himself. Surely, his fellow poet would be impressed. Enzo had never thought of having his poems published, but why not? It would be wonderful to see his heartfelt words in print. Maybe this club would help him do that.

The student who would lead the club was not what Enzo expected, though he wasn't sure exactly what he had expected. She was tall and rather oddly dressed, in a sort of shawl over a long, flowing skirt. Her dark brown hair was pulled back in a French braid with a single rose woven into it. As the students entered, she played softly on what looked like a small harp, humming in a sweet, quiet voice. The effect was charming; Enzo felt his heart leap before she even said a word.

The girl stopped strumming and introduced herself. "Ciao, all. My name is Erato. You can call me Era. I go to the International School, but I'm new to this neighborhood. I wanted to lead this club so I could meet kids who love poetry like I do. Your school's Activity Council liked the fact that I've had some poetry published, so they agreed to give it a try." Era held up her little harp. "I started off with music because it helps me tune into my feelings. And poetry is all about feelings! Let's start by finding out who's here. Tell me your names and why you want to write poetry."

As the kids introduced themselves, Gina watched Enzo

with amused dismay. *Oh dear*, she thought, *he's a goner already! Poor Jordan. I hope she didn't think she'd be the one to last.*

Era shared her plans for the club. "We'll start by reading classic romantic poetry. How many of you are already poets?" Three raised their hands. Enzo waved his arm eagerly, setting off chuckles around the room. The other two were more tentative about it. Era invited them to bring in their poems to share. "It'll encourage everyone to write and give us a chance to start critiquing each other's work." One student asked Era to read some of her poems, which she did.

Gina didn't know much about poetry and she'd never tried to write any. She wasn't sure why she'd let Enzo talk her into coming with him. He certainly did enough writing for both of them! But as she listened to Era's verse, she could tell that it was different. Kind of formal and, she was sure, much better than Enzo's little rhymes. Maybe he'd learn something from Era. Maybe she would, too.

At the end of the session, Enzo bolted to the front of the room to talk to Era. He introduced himself again. "Hi, I'm Enzo. I've written lots of poems. I write them for people and give them away, but I have a notebook of copies at home. I'll bring it next week. I think I'm really going to like this club. And I think your poems are really great—maybe the best I've ever heard!"

Era smiled. She knew, of course, that her poetry was excellent, but still felt flattered by his praise. He was handsome, and his unguarded enthusiasm was appealing. *Hmm... Maybe this assignment won't be so bad after all!* "Thanks, Enzo. I'm eager to read yours. What kinds of poems do you write?"

Gina, waiting for Enzo by the door, was surprised to see a trace of blush creep into Enzo's cheeks as he answered, "Love poems, mostly. I write a lot of love poems. Love inspires me, and I just have to write about it."

"Well, now I really am looking forward to reading them! They should fit perfectly with what I have planned for the next few weeks. See you soon!"

Enzo was barely outside the building before he asked Gina what rhymes with "shawl."

All that week Enzo couldn't stop talking about Era. He'd already written not one, but several poems to her. Jordan was history.

Gina was surprised and a little wary. This was new territory for Enzo. Not only several poems to the same girl, but each about something different—her hair, her clothes, her singing voice, her friendliness. Even her courage for moving to a new place and leading a club full of strangers!

"Do you think she'll like them, Gina? She's such a great poet. And such an amazing person. What if she doesn't like them?"

"You've never worried about that before. Why so concerned this time?" Gina asked, but Enzo only looked away. This was different, Gina realized, and she didn't like it one bit. Enzo's crushes had always been fleeting and, if not exactly frivolous, certainly superficial. His heart would tug at one girl's style, another's kindheartedness, another's cleverness, but never the girl as a whole. Yet he seemed to love everything he knew (which, after all, wasn't much!) about Era. Gina had to admit it. She was a little jealous, plain and simple.

The next Saturday, Enzo brought his notebook of poems to the club. He read aloud, but with uncharacteristic shyness:

Laughter like a sparkling brook
Bubbles up each time I look
At your happy, smiling face.

We laugh together and I know
That life is better when we go
Together through the rain and snow.

Another student shared some poems as well. Era led the conversation from a simple noting of rhymes and meter to a deeper look at themes and images in romantic poetry. Again, after the meeting, Gina waited as Enzo approached Era and offered to loan her his notebook. "The last few, the ones in the back, I wrote this week. I hope you like them."

"Thanks, Enzo. I'm sure I will," she cooed, smiling coyly.

"Maybe we can talk about them next time."

Watching from the doorway, Gina didn't like what she saw. She couldn't hear the words, but wasn't Era acting a little too friendly and encouraging? Did she really twirl a wisp of hair around her fingers and flutter her eyelashes in Enzo's direction?

That night, curled up in a soft chair in the little villa where she'd rented a room, Era read Enzo's poems. They didn't all include names, but they were obviously written for girls he liked and it was obviously many different girls. Some poems made her wince with their sing-songy rhythms and awkward phrases. But some showed hints of originality and creative structure. He did have potential and, what's more, he was cute! As she got to the new poems in the back, she realized, with a flush of pleasure, that they were written for her. After all, who else wore a shawl, even if rhyming it with *crawl* was less than inspired? And this one—he actually referred to her as his Muse! *Oh dear, does he suspect? No, that's ridiculous. It's just a figure of speech.* She noticed something else. These later poems were better than the earlier ones. She was already inspiring him to improve! One thing was clear: *I am Enzo's new crush!* She giggled. *OK,* she thought, *I can use that to complete my mission and have a little harmless fun at the same time!*

At the next club meeting, after reading some Keats and Petrarch, Era compared the poem Enzo had read aloud last time to one of his recent ones, written for her. She recited,

>"*Soul to match my soul,*
>*Heart to match my heart,*
>*She appears from nowhere,*
>*Mystery surrounding,*
>*Just to take my part.*
>
>*I in turn, responding,*
>*Seek to become whole,*
>*Finding what's inside me—*
>*Heart to match her heart,*

Soul to match her soul."

The group applauded; Era smiled warmly at Enzo. "See how much Enzo's poetry has improved in just a couple of weeks? The less obvious rhyme scheme and personal tone make the emotions feel deeper and more genuine, don't you think?"

This time, Era noticed, Gina didn't wait for Enzo at the end of the session. Enzo headed straight for Era, grinning adoringly and acting surprisingly shy. "Enzo, you really do have a knack for verse. If you keep improving like this, you'll have girls falling at your feet! Did you really write those last poems for me?"

I've got him eating out of my hand, she thought. *I'll be tasting pear sorbet on Mount Helicon in no time. But, really, what's the rush?*

Era and Enzo parted ways. As Era made her way down the hall to leave the building, the door to the girl's restroom opened and an arm reached out to grab Era and pull her inside. Shocked, Era whirled around to face her oldest sister! Calliope had a death grip on her and a look of fierce irritation on her face.

"Calli!" What in Zeus' name are you doing here? I didn't call for you!"

"I know you didn't. But apparently, you need help! Mother snatched me away from my own mission to come here and shake some sense into you. I'm no happier about it than you are, I assure you!"

"Mother did **what**? Why? My mission's going just fine! I have Enzo right where I want him!"

"Yes, and it seems you're enjoying yourself a little too much! 'Why, Enzo, you really do have a knack for verse. Did you really write those poems for little old **me**?' I can see why Mother's upset—I'm gagging here!"

"What do you mean? I'm just inspiring him. Can I help it if he adores me?"

"Well, Mother seems to think you can, and says to tell you that you'd better! She was muttering something about how you're 'too much like your father,' and I don't think she meant it as a compliment [1]! She sent me to tell you to get over yourself and focus on your mission. You're supposed to be helping him develop his emotions, so he can write serious poetry, and instead you're fawning and flirting and leading him on."

"But he's getting better! His poems are much better than before I came, already! And Daddy can't help it that women love him. It's a curse we share—being irresistible!"

"Oh, **please**!" Calliope rolled her eyes. "I won't even waste my breath on that one. Besides, if we start fighting, Mother's sure to see. I suggest you figure out another way to help your adoring poet, because this way isn't making Mother happy, and none of us will let you forget it if we lose our pear sorbet forever because of you! Got it?"

"OK. But he's got it bad for me. What am I supposed to do?"

"Well the way I hear it, he's not exactly famous for long-term commitments. Steer him toward someone else. Simple!" And with that, Calliope vanished.

Era slumped to the floor. *What just happened? How dare Calliope charge into my mission and tell me what to do? How dare Mother send her?* But she shied away from that thought as soon as it crossed her mind. Mother could dare anything she pleased! Even more unsettling was the thought that Mother was watching them so closely. *"Too much fun?"* But she was the Muse of romantic poetry! Of course Enzo was attracted to her, and flirting was as natural to her as breathing. What did Mother expect? She was supposed to inspire, and Enzo was, clearly, inspired! *And what about Enzo?* How could she discourage his crush without discouraging his writing? It would break his poor, lovesick heart! It would be a tragedy for the poor boy! *That's it,* she thought. *Melpomene—the Muse of tragedy! Maybe she can help me figure out what to do.*

Era tapped out the sisters' code—first the middle finger on her left hand to signal Melpomene, the third-born sister, and then her left thumb, to tell Mel that the fifth-born Muse was calling her. Almost before she finished, Mel took shape next to her on the restroom floor. "What's up, Era?" asked Mel. "I should thank you for giving me a break from my kid. She's wearing me down! But I can't stay long. We're sort of at a critical point, and I had to tell her I needed to find a bathroom. What do you know—I was telling the truth!"

Era sputtered as she filled Mel in on the surprising developments, still indignant at Calliope's interference. "So you see," she concluded, "rejecting Enzo is going to break his heart, and he's only human. That's where you come in. I thought you might have some ideas about how to ease the tragedy for him."

"Era, you are **so** full of yourself!" Mel bristled.

"Full of myself? I'm just doing my job here! Why send me if I'm not supposed to act like myself?"

Mel closed her eyes, took a breath, and held her hands up in front of her. "OK, let's take a moment. We don't dare fight with Mother watching, and it won't help either of us get our jobs done."

"You're right. But what do I do now?"

"I'm sure Enzo is crazy about you. How could he resist? After all, you are a goddess—he's never met anyone like you before. But he's liked lots of girls. There must be something you can do to put him off; someone else you can help him shift his affections to, or see you shifting yours to."

"Hmm. Now that I think about it, I did notice something about his poems. In the early ones he sounds like a magpie—attracted to one shiny thing about one girl after another. He likes one girl's smile, another one's sense of humor, and so on. But the new ones, written for me, are about different things, like maybe he's ready to see a girl as a whole person."

"Well, there you go! Look over the early poems and find someone who has several qualities he likes. With your talent for romance, it should be a snap to make him like her instead."

"You might be onto something. There's a girl in the club that seems to be his friend. She's funny and smart and quite pretty. In fact, she doesn't seem very happy that he's focused on me. Maybe I could get Enzo to notice her as more than a buddy. But how? I'm telling you, right now he's pretty stuck on me."

"How about this? Create a little drama. Can you get someone to flirt with this other girl in front of him? Or flirt with someone else yourself? Maybe that would discourage him, without putting him down directly. It could backfire, I suppose, but it's all I've got."

"I'll think about it. It won't be easy, getting him to prefer a mortal girl to, well, **me**! It might require some drama. But then, I'm almost as good at creating drama as you are!"

The sisters wished each other luck. Mel disappeared, and Era left the restroom, deep in thought.

Enzo made his way home, thrilled with Era's attention and praise and already shaping another poem in his mind. Up ahead, he saw Gina. *Is she waiting for me? Good! I can't wait to tell her about this! But wait, she's not alone.* Gina was talking to a guy with a bike, who looked familiar. *Is that Dominic? He doesn't live around here.* He was a nice enough guy, but what was he doing with Gina? Enzo caught up and greeted them, but the conversation stalled. When Enzo said, "I'm heading home. Coming, Gina?" she shrugged, waved at Dominic, and joined Enzo.

"Gina, you won't believe what she said about me!" Enzo began when Dominic was out of range. "She said my poems are getting really good, and that…"

"That's great, Enzo," she interrupted. "I've got to go. See you."

What a strange day, thought Enzo. *First Era loves my poems and seems to like me, too, and then Gina doesn't have time for me. She always has time for me!* But he was too happy to wonder for long. He sprinted across the street, into his villetta, and straight to his room to write.

In the days that followed, Enzo saw Dominic talking to Gina several times at school. Dominic even walked his bike home with them a couple of times, though he lived in the other direction. He was friendly, but he didn't talk much. For that matter, Gina was quiet, too. Enzo cheerfully carried the conversation with chatter about his latest poems and the amazing Era. Thursday, Enzo was just finishing a story about his little brother's mischief when they reached Gina's house. He looked up and caught Gina's eye. She stared at him intensely and subtly nodded her head toward his house across the street. *Is Gina telling me to get lost? What's going on here?* Startled and a little hurt, he waved lamely and headed home. When he glanced back from his door, the two were sitting on her front step and... what? Were they holding hands?

Enzo finished his homework and took out his poetry journal, eager to start a new poem for Era. He'd been thinking about the rose in Era's hair all afternoon. That was a good place to start.

Bright and sparkling like a ruby in straw...

No, that wouldn't do.

I'll bring you roses to cover your tresses,
You'll know my heart without any guesses...

No good. The words weren't pouring out as they usually did. Every time he tried to concentrate, the image of Gina and Dominic holding hands popped into his mind and distracted him. He was annoyed with himself and, oddly, with Gina as well. Why had she acted like she didn't want him around? And why should he care if Dominic wanted to hold her hand? He shook his head. *I'm a poet. I needed to focus. I need to let go of everything else and tune into "my Muse."* Words had never failed him before, and Era inspired him more than anyone. So why did his mind keep wandering, even when he tried to think about her?

By the poetry club meeting on Saturday, Enzo was upset. He hadn't written anything good in days. When Era asked who had new work to share, he looked down at his shoes rather than waving his hand.

"Enzo, nothing from you today?" Era asked.

"Not really. Thomas read some last week. Maybe he has more."

Thomas did. It wasn't very good, Enzo thought, but Era praised him lavishly and shared one of her poems with a similar rhyme scheme. Enzo was uneasy. *What's happening to me?* He felt confused and flustered, and both feelings were unusual for him. *Maybe it's writer's block.* He'd read somewhere that all writers get blocked eventually. *Maybe I've been writing so much that I've earned my first writer's block! Could that be it? I'll bet Era can tell me.* Lost in thought, Enzo was startled to hear Era dismiss the group and ask Thomas to stay behind. As Enzo headed toward her for their usual after-meeting chat, he saw Era turn away from him and gush about Thomas' new poems with more excitement than Enzo thought they deserved. She tossed her head and laughed her high, twinkly laugh at Thomas. She touched his shoulder. Thomas seemed tongue-tied, but grinned foolishly and nodded at everything Era said. *How can this be? She really likes my poems, and was so happy that they were for her. Doesn't she feel the same way about me? Why is she treating Thomas the way she treated me just last week?*

As Enzo left the room, Era flirted with Thomas with half of her attention. With the other half she wondered, feeling vague pangs of guilt, *will it work?*

He had to find Gina. He had to talk to her. He could tell her everything and she'd help him feel like himself and sort things out, like she always did. Enzo dashed out of the room. He sprinted from the building and down the street in the direction Gina would have taken home. *There she is.* But Dominic was with her again! He must have waited through the whole club meeting to walk her home! Enzo was gaining on them, but as he approached he stopped short. *When did Gina's hair get so long and shimmery?* It glinted in the afternoon sun. She turned toward Dominic, and the smile she flashed him was dazzling—full of mischief and warmth. *When did she get so pretty?* Enzo had known her forever, but he'd never noticed before how graceful she was when she walked, or realized how much he counted on her. Nobody else knew him as well or stuck by him the way she did. He felt his heart pound. Wait a minute. What's going on here? Could it be? *Of course, that's it! All this time, all these girls I've written poems for, were all just practice! It was Gina all along!* Why hadn't he seen it sooner? But this was perfect, really, because now that he was improving as a poet, he could write her a really, really

85

good poem. She'd be so impressed and happy! Enzo could hardly wait to get home. *No more writer's block for me!*

The next morning, Enzo loped across the street toward Gina's villetta. He was excited, but nervous, too. *Why am I nervous?* He'd always been as comfortable with Gina as with his own family, and he'd given dozens of girls poems before. It was a good poem, he was sure. Maybe his best. He especially liked that dancing image in the last stanza, because it led into the perfect closing gesture. At the end of the poem, he'd written a note inviting her to go to the spring dance with him! She'd be so surprised and happy, and it would be good to get things settled between them before Dominic had any troublesome ideas....

"Hi, Enzo! I didn't know you were coming over. What's up?"

Before a grinning Enzo could pull the poem from his pocket and give it to her, Dominic popped his head out from the kitchen.

"Hey, Enzo. Who are you taking to the spring dance? That girl from the poetry club? Gina just said she'd go with me. Isn't that great?"

A moment of stunned silence passed. "Ah, sure, great. That's great. Is that great, Gina?" Enzo stumbled over his words.

"Sure is!" she replied, too happy to notice the stricken look on Enzo's face right away. "Mom said we can have some kids over to eat before the dance. Maybe you and Era could come. Enzo? Are you OK, Enzo?"

"Sure. Fine. But I just remembered something. I have to get home. We'll talk later. You guys have fun. Ciao." He bolted out the door and home as fast as he could, furious with himself, with Gina, with Dominic, with Era, with just about everyone. *How could I have gotten it so wrong? Why didn't I figure out sooner that it was Gina I cared about? How could my timing be so bad? How could Gina want Dominic instead of me?* Back in his room, he pulled the poem from his pocket. It was his best one yet. He knew it. Now she'd never read it. He tore it into tiny snippets and let them sift through his fingers into the trash. He threw himself on his bed to wallow in anguish.

Still, as Enzo lay across his bed indulging the misery of his situation, he realized that the ill-fatedness of it all had a certain dramatic, star-crossed appeal, and he reached for his pen....

A Cruel Archer by Enzo Moretti
You're a cruel archer, Cupid.
I thought you a light, happy spirit,
'Til you loosed your arrow and pierced my heart.
Happy I was to feel love's sting,
Sure that you'd sent my arrow's mate
Straight into the heart of my heart's desire.

But you, in what meanness of spirit,
Had other plans.
The arrow you sent to my love
Had a match aimed at another's waiting chest.

Now I can only watch and sigh,
A victim of your unkind joke,
While the one my heart beats for clings to another.

I wonder if my arrow's mate will ever fly
And, if it flew, could I ever love its target?

Footnotes
1. While Zeus and Mnemosyne had nine daughters in common, they were not married. Zeus was not the faithful type; he had many wives and many affairs. Here, Erato's tendency to flirt has angered Mnemosyne by reminding her of Zeus's fickle ways.

CHAPTER 6
MELPOMENE'S MISSION: A HERO'S STORY?

Melpomene, you are the Muse of Tragedy. I've chosen for you a thirteen-year-old girl in Sierra Leone, West Africa, whose ancestors were victims of slavery. She has potential to be a strong leader, a voice for compassion and healing. But she lacks knowledge and appreciation of her heritage. She has a chance, through a school assignment, to connect to her past, and come to understand that tragedy can create heroes, large and small. You will help her make the most of this opportunity.

Freetown, Sierra Leone
Mardea crashed through the door and slammed her books on the kitchen table.

"Another term project," she wailed, in response to her mother's startled expression. The school term had barely begun and Mardea was already discouraged. "Secondary school is murder! This time our history and English teachers ganged up on us. They're in it together and there's no getting around it! It counts as half our grade in both classes."

"Come have a snack. Tell me about this nightmare project." Mother patted the chair next to her. "It can't be that bad. Interdisciplinary projects are more work for teachers, but they can really help students make connections."

"Oh, please, not the teacher-talk," Mardea whined, rolling her eyes. "You know I hate that! It's a report we have to give out loud, in front of everyone, about 'An Ancestor Who Influenced Me.' I don't even **know** my ancestors except Gramps and Gran Trye. How could any of those dead people influence me?"

Mother stroked Mardea's short, tangled hair. "Well, maybe this is your chance to find out. Sounds like it could be interesting. Do you have any ideas?"

"How could I? They're a bunch of dead people I don't know anything about. What could be more boring than shuffling through old newspapers about people who lived a long time ago?"

"Hmm… you might be surprised. What about that story of our ancestor from Mendeland, who was supposedly sold into slavery in the 1800s? You've heard your grandparents mention him. Maybe you can find out what happened to him. We'd help, you know."

"But what does that have to do with me? I know it bothers you and Dad. Every time it comes up, you get mad. But that was a long time ago."

Mother paused before answering, her finger tracing an invisible circle on the tabletop. "You're right; we do get mad when we hear that story. Everything about the way human beings have been bought and sold, through the centuries, is maddening. It still happens in some places. Young people should be angry about it, too! It touches us all; we all carry some of the anger and humiliation of those experiences."

"Maybe you do, but not me! Fine, whatever. I guess since I have to find an interesting ancestor, he's as good a place to start as any. I'll call Gran. Do you think Dad would get me into the library at Fourah Bay University? If I have to go digging through ancient history, I suppose that's the best place."

"I'm sure he would. Ask him when he gets home."

Dad agreed right away, looking so pleased that Mardea almost felt bad about not showing more interest in his work. The next Saturday found Mardea slumped in a chair in the library's reference room, slogging through musty old books, ledgers, and records on microfiche film. Dust motes floated in the warm light from the windows. The humid air lulled her, and the pages began to blur in front of her. *How will I find anything in this mass of pointless details?* She rubbed her nose to ward off a sneeze. Mardea loved her grandparents and their eagerness to help her, but they hadn't given her much to work with—just some ancient stories that got them all worked up. They had a village, a vague date, and a name. They weren't even sure if it was his real name or a nickname. It was a place to start and the librarians were almost too helpful, returning often with "one more thing you might try." But her first attempt at research had gone nowhere. She'd been at it for almost two hours!

A young librarian approached Mardea holding a slim picture book. "This probably won't help you find your ancestor, but it's a favorite of mine that I show to anyone interested in the Middle Passage slave trade. I thought you might like to see it."

"Thanks." Mardea reached for the book, welcoming a distraction. *From Slave Ship to Freedom Road*, by Julius Lester [1], the cover read. She began to thumb through the pages, and was instantly struck by the pictures. Horror replaced boredom as she examined the stark, powerful paintings, each more disturbing than the last. She sat up straight and began to read, feeling first disbelief, and then anger, rise in her. After a page showing slaves stacked like sardines on sleeping shelves on a lower deck of a ship, Mardea slammed the book shut and pushed it across the table, as far from her as possible. Her stomach felt queasy. *Why did she show me that book? It's horrible! It's her favorite? How could it be anyone's favorite? How could she think I'd 'like to see it?' How could anyone "like" this? And it's not even getting me any closer to finding my ancestor.*

Mardea reached for the next dusty ledger, this time

almost glad to return to the mundane task at hand as relief from the haunting words and images. She tried, not very successfully, to put Lester's book out of her mind.

After another half hour of getting nowhere, Mardea sighed dramatically, about to give up. It wasn't quite four o'clock; maybe she'd still have time for a movie with friends. But then something jumped out at her from an old church register—"Burna," the name Gran had told her. It wasn't much, but there it was! She had to admit, it gave her a little shiver to see it in print. The name was right. The place was right. He was married in 1827, it said, to a woman named Aissa. So now she had two names to look for. With a little surge of energy, she began to track both names through the village census records.

Her excitement didn't last long. An hour later she climbed into her father's car, complaining. "Dad, you'll never believe this! I thought I'd found Burna—right name, right dates, right village. And he **was** taken by a Portuguese slave trader in the 1830s. But get this—I couldn't find anything more, except that his wife died in 1841 and she had no children! So how could he be our ancestor?"

"Maybe he had another wife," Dad countered. "They did sometimes, back then. I don't know. He could still be the right one. My friend Tamba can show you some other sources, next time you're there. It's hard tracing back that many generations, but he's good at it. Don't give up. You might be on the right track."

Sometimes her parents' calm encouragement was so annoying! They just didn't get that not everyone loved school and studying like they did. "Stupid report," Mardea mumbled. Aloud, she said, "I wasted the whole afternoon, and got nowhere. All it's doing is making me mad about slavery, too! Dad, have you seen this?" Something had made her check out Lester's book and take it with her. She waved it at him. "It's full of horrible pictures of what it was like for slaves in the ships and on the plantations. They were chained to each other on the ship and jammed together on shelves to sleep." Mardea's face reddened, and her voice rose as she described what she'd read. "Their masters sold their children for money, and sometimes they never saw them again! How could they stand it? Why did they put up with it? When they died on the ships, the slavers tossed them in the water like yesterday's trash! Who would **do** something like that?"

"It's awful, I know." Her father reached over the steering wheel to stroke her arm. "But at least you found a story from history that has you thinking and feeling. That's good. I'm sure it's what your teachers hoped would happen. Start writing about that, and keep researching."

The rest of the ride home was silent, as Mardea moped over both the ugliness of what she had learned and the meager results of her effort.

At school two weeks later, Mrs. Tarawali introduced a new student. She was a violet-eyed girl, about Mardea's height but slimmer, with hair so blonde it seemed to shimmer. She wore the strangest boots Mardea had ever seen, and a funny-looking headband that looked like it was made of weeds. "Class, this is… Tell me your name again, dear."

"Melpomene."

"I'm sorry. Help me. Melpo…"

"Just call me Mel."

"Mel just moved to Freetown. Her parents work at the Greek Embassy. She'll be with us for the rest of the term. We're glad to have you, Mel. You may sit over there." She pointed at an empty desk in the row next to Mardea's. "Mardea, would you help Mel get settled? I was telling Mel about our term project. But since she's getting a late start and we might not have records here to trace her ancestors, I've taken her suggestion to let her work with one of you. Mardea, you've been having some trouble pinning down your ancestor, and Mel lives near you. How about letting her help you? I think that will work fine."

"Yes, Ma'am." Mardea couldn't refuse, but she didn't like this new arrangement at all. *Terrific,* she thought. *Now I have this weird girl on my hands on top of the dumb project to do! And no choice about either.*

Mel slid into her desk and waved at Mardea. "I live right down your street," she whispered. "Mrs. T. told me where you live. I could come over and you could show me what you've got so far. We'll figure out how I can help."

"OK, I guess. I'm not getting anywhere but mad on my own. How about tomorrow after school?"

"Great."

The next afternoon, the two girls sat on Mardea's bed eating mangoes. While Mel nibbled neatly at the orange flesh, Mardea let the sweet, sticky juice drip down her chin. Mardea commented, "So, Mel. I never heard that name before, for a girl."

"It's short for Melpomene"

"Mel... what?"

"You know, Melpom... Don't you people...? Never mind. Weird mother. Something about Greek goddesses. You know how moms are!"

"Do I ever! And what's with the boots and that headband thing? Are they some new fad kids are wearing in Greece?"

"Oh, these? Just my signature look, I guess. You know, something to help me feel like myself, while my family moves around. Do you like them?"

"Uh, I guess. They're sort of funky."

"Show me what you've got so far on this ancestor thing."

"It's not much. I hit a dead end. You'll see it there. Mostly it just made me mad."

"Let's see." Mel skimmed Mardea's draft, eyes widening as she read Mardea's comments about the slave trade.

"Wow! You really are mad about what you read! Your handwriting even gets all squiggly here." Mel pointed to a paragraph on the page. "This is good stuff, though. This Lester guy's book really set you off, didn't it?"

"Well, look at it!" Mardea snapped, pulling out the book and showing it to Mel. "That part I quote is right at the beginning, about dropping dead slaves overboard like empty wine barrels, but with eyes that cry and mouths that scream. Doesn't it make you mad? Who could **not** get mad?"

"I see what you mean. It's terrible." Mel dropped her mango pit in the wastebasket, then stood at the window, trying to shake off the horrifying images. "I could help with your research. Maybe between us, we could find out more about this Burna. When can we go back to the library?"

"I don't know. It feels kind of pointless. It seems like no one cared about people after they were taken for slaves. They disappear from the records. Maybe we should just forget it and write about slavery instead. I could say I might have had an ancestor who was a slave."

I can see this won't be easy, thought Mel, already annoyed by Mardea's whining and lack of motivation. "I don't mean to be rude, but couldn't lots of kids here say the same thing? And it's supposed to be about a specific ancestor. We can't give up already—it's my grade too, you know!"

Mardea rolled her eyes. "Oh, alright. I can't afford a bad grade, either. My dad knows everyone at the University library. His friend said he'd show me some more sources. Can you go over the weekend?"

"Sure. I just got here. I don't have any plans."

Back at the library on Saturday, Mardea's father's friend gave them some tips and led them to more records. But even with two of them, almost an hour's work had turned up nothing useful. Mardea jiggled her foot, tapped her pencil on the table, and kept looking at the clock. A stack of ledgers and several newspapers lay scattered on the table around the girls, searched and discarded.

"See what I mean?" Mardea asked Mel. "Nothing! And the first draft is due in a week! What are we supposed to do?"

Mel waved off Mardea's complaint and held up a finger. "Hold on—I think I just found something. Look at this—could this be your Burna?" She pushed a stained ledger toward Mardea, pointing to a line near the bottom of the page.

"Let me see that." Mel studied the paper. "It's a birth record. 'Mother: Isata of Barthurst, Father: Burna, blacksmith and farmer from Bo.' The baby's name is Burna, too! Born in 1835. That fits! He could have had a baby with this Isata woman and then been captured after that. Dad said men sometimes had two wives then, but I didn't find any marriage record. Uh-oh, wait a minute—oh, this is bad."

Mardea shuffled through the books littering the table. "I

saw something in this other book..." She unearthed a newer-looking volume and rifled through the pages. "Here it is. It says men were sometimes turned over to black slave traders as punishment for adultery. Maybe this woman who had the baby wasn't married to Burna, so they punished him by making him a slave! Just great! What a wonderful 'influence' this guy's turning out to be!" Mardea dropped her head into her hands in frustration.

Growing more irritated by the minute, Mel forced herself to be encouraging. "Still, he could be your great-great-great-great grandfather or something," she coaxed, following the entry through the ledger. She tapped the page with excitement. "Get this! This baby grew up to be a blacksmith too, and told everyone that his father was part of the slave mutiny on the *Amistad* [2]! Do you know about the *Amistad*? I've heard a little about it. We talked about it in my Mort... I mean 19th Century—History class. It was a big deal—changing laws about slaves and all that."

"Do I know about it? You can't live in Freetown and **not** know about it! There's a museum here and everything. Every school kid goes there. I never paid much attention. It just seemed like one of those things kids are supposed to be excited about, because the grown-ups are." Mardea looked up, a faint hint of interest lighting her eyes. "Do you think my Burna could really have been a freedom fighter? That would be cool. I could write about that!"

"Why not? Let's find some books on the *Amistad* rebellion." *OK*, Mel thought as they headed for the stacks. *Maybe now we're getting somewhere.*

The next day, as the girls sprawled on Mardea's bed poring over books about the Amistad, Mardea let out a wail.

"Oh, **no**! I was finally getting excited about having a freedom fighter for an ancestor, but listen to this! Two slaves died at the very beginning of the battle to take over the ship, and one was Burna! That means he didn't even make it to America! He didn't live to see the courts free them, or even know they won the battle and took the ship." Mardea thumped the book with her fist. "You know how hard we've looked for more details about the battle; there's just nothing more here!"

Mel winced. Mardea's griping grated on her like the screech of a Harpy [3].

Mardea ranted on. "After all the trouble we had tracing this guy, I thought we were onto something good. But his body probably ended up in the ocean and we'll never know whether he even put up a fight. So much for a hero's story to tell. What a stupid assignment!" Mardea threw down the book, and slumped in defeat.

"Oh, for the love of Zeus!" mumbled Mel. Even the most annoying of her sisters didn't irritate her like Mardea. She actually felt a twinge of loneliness for them. And while losing pear sorbet might not be anything like the tragedy that the *Amistad* rebellion represented, she realized she would hate to be responsible for depriving her sisters of the pleasure of it forever, which, after all, is a very long time when you're immortal! Mel sighed and composed herself to try again. "It's your ancestor, but it's our report. Think about it—You could probably write a mushy little bit about how your Mom influences you by taking good care of you, or you like your grandma's family stories. But you've still got something here. Like they say, 'When life gives you lemons, make lemonade.'"

"Lemonade? What could this possibly have to do with lemonade?" Mardea asked, looking puzzled and disgusted at once.

"OK, bad choice of words. Wrong 'they.' How about 'When life gives you cassava, make tapioca pudding?' It just means, when you have problems, make the best of it. Your ancestor was on the *Amistad*, for heaven's sake! He was one of fewer than fifty slaves there. And the fact that he didn't live to be freed, or even to see what happened, only makes it more tragic! What more do you need? That's bound to be better than anything the other kids found."

Mel glanced at Mardea to see if her words were having any effect. Mardea's scowl softened, and she seemed to be at least considering what Mel had to say. Mel knew she was wheedling and she hated it, but the tantalizing thought of eating pear sorbet with her sisters at the end of the mission kept her going. And, really, this whole *Amistad* thing was as impressively sad and exciting as the stories of the greats back home; even the exaggerated versions told at banquets. Then she had an idea.

"Let's look one more time. If we can't find more facts about the *Amistad*, how about some fiction? Lots of made-up stories come from family histories or memories passed from parents to their kids. Who says those aren't true?" Mel paced as she talked, excited by her own words. "If we keep looking, maybe we'll find something more we can use. Some of the *Amistad* slaves came back to Africa after the trials were over, right? Someone around here must have written stories about them. We'll look at fiction instead. Let's try the school library's computer catalog."

Mardea trudged to the computer on her desk, logged on to the school website, and navigated her way to the catalog. "I don't have any better ideas. Who'd have thought those library lessons in primary school would actually come in handy?"

Mel looked over Mardea's shoulder. "Look," she said, pointing. "Here are four titles. And this one looks promising. It's by someone who's great-whatever grandfather lived through the whole *Amistad* thing and came back home to tell about it. Let's go!"

Later that afternoon, after a trip to the library's fiction section, the girls sat cross-legged on the floor. Mardea nudged Mel and pointed out a section in the book she was cradling.

"Here's where they talk about the fight. It says that one of the two who died early in the battle was trying to disarm an *Amistad* crew member, so another slave could get to the ship's captain and kill him! It doesn't say how the second one died, but it does say he was against the plan to take over the ship. But the names are made up. How am I supposed to know which one was Burna?" She slammed the book shut and shook her head. "That's just great! My ancestor might have died being a hero for freedom, or he might have been a coward hiding in a corner! And the report's due tomorrow!"

"Still, I think we can use it," said Mel, trying hard to keep her voice calm. "Think about it this way. You get to decide what you believe. You can choose to believe that your ancestor was the first one, who died fighting. Maybe the second one got into the fight too, once it was happening. Or maybe he didn't want to fight because he was worried about what their dying would mean for their families back home." Mel reached into the bag she'd dropped beside the bed, and pulled out a book. "You know that book about slaves you showed me? The one by Julius Lester? I checked it out and found something. Here, listen to this part:

"'Who is more heroic?—slaves like Nat Turner, Sojourner Truth, and Frederick Douglass, who fought back, or an anonymous slave holding on to his hat as white as cotton. We do not have to choose. Heroism has many faces...' [4]

"Whichever one was related to you, and whatever really happened to him, he was part of history and looking for him got you interested in this amazing story. Isn't that enough influence to make your teacher happy?"

"What makes you so cheery? You have an answer for everything! Are you always like this?" snapped Mardea, tired and annoyed.

"I've just been around, you know, and I know some things." Mel was having a little trouble holding herself together.

"Figures. You embassy kids always think you're such big stuff! You're not, you know. And besides, **your** ancestors probably weren't stolen from their homes and turned into slaves and dumped in the ocean and worked to death on plantations! And they probably weren't heroes, either!"

*That does it! **My** family, not heroes? If she had any clue...* Mel clenched her fists, dangerously close to losing her temper and dropping her cover. "You know what? You're right. All **my** ancestors ever did was..." With a huge effort of will, she abandoned that dangerous train of thought and settled for exasperation instead. "I give up! Maybe I'll just leave you to write your stupid report alone."

"Fine. You do that. It'll be better without you anyway."

Mel stormed out of the room and slammed the door. *That girl is so stubborn! Angry and helpless and determined to fail! Who cares? I don't have to stick around and get the bad grade!*

But she'd no more than hit the sidewalk when she realized that her temper had gotten the best of her. It wasn't just about a bad grade. She couldn't afford to mess up her mission. It wasn't only the prospect of a life without pear sorbet. Her sisters would never forgive her. But even more than that, she realized that she really wanted to help Mardea see things differently.

Great! she thought. *What now?*

Of course, she knew what she had to do. She had to call for help. Reluctantly, she scrolled through the roll of sisters in her mind, trying to figure out who would help most and gloat least. *Not Calliope, that's for sure. She's oldest, even though it's only by a few days* [5], *and she always thinks she's the boss of us. And not Euterpe. Mardea's right about one thing— too much cheeriness can be annoying. Maybe Thalia. She always lightens things up without too much sweetness, and she's pretty smart. OK, here goes.*

Mel ducked into a deserted side street where she wouldn't be seen, and tapped her right middle finger once, followed by her left middle finger.

She didn't have long to wait. Thalia appeared beside her, a little out of breath.

"What's the scene, Mel-po-mene?" Thalia asked, deliberately mispronouncing Mel's name to tease her. "This had better be good. I'm in the middle of my mission too, you know. My kid's a natural, but he's got no guts! I don't know what I'm going to do with him."

"You think you've got problems! Mardea is the most infuriating person I've ever met. First she can't find her ancestor. Then she's too angry about the whole slavery thing to keep looking. Then when I practically drop the guy in her lap, she's unhappy because he might not be some big hero." Mel stopped pacing and threw her hands up in a "Do you believe it?" gesture. "And now she's mad at me for trying to help her see the bright side! How do you handle someone like that? You just can't win!"

"Wow! Sounds like you've met your match for drama!" Thalia chuckled, patting Mel's back to calm her. "At least she's upset about something important. I can't think of much that's more tragic than slavery, and we've seen our share of tragedies around Mount Olympus! I don't think even I could find something funny in that. Give her a break, OK? You're not always the easiest to deal with yourself, you know? We all have to complete our missions, if we ever want to taste you-know-what again. Take a deep breath, get back over there, and talk some sense into her! I need to get back to Minnesota, of all places!"

Thalia's common sense cut through Mel's frustration. She sighed and shrugged. "I guess you're right. I remember how disappointed I was, when our good-for-nothing brother Ares turned out to be a coward instead of the great champion I pictured in my head [6]. Maybe that's how she's feeling about her ancestor. I just wish she didn't make me so mad! I'll try nudging her one more time."

"You do that, sis. Meanwhile, I'm back to the soggy, muddy North Country. They need some jokes there, especially this time of year!" Thalia disappeared as quickly as she'd arrived.

Mel headed back to Mardea's house, resolved to get her back on track. It took some doing—first an apology (it was hard not to make it sound grudging), then a reminder of the grade at stake for both of them, and finally a pep talk about how important the *Amistad* was and how exciting it was that Mardea's ancestor was part of the story. *Maybe not inspiring,* Mel thought, *but I think I'm wearing her down.* Mardea finally gave in.

"OK, you win. I'll write about Burna. Maybe it wasn't such a stupid assignment. It is kind of cool that my ancestor was on the *Amistad*, even with all I don't know. It really could turn out to be the best story in the class."

"That's more like it!" Mel replied, already anticipating the cool, luscious tang of pear sorbet on her tongue. "Lots of what you already have is OK. You just need to work in what you know about Burna. Let the anger work for you. After all, who can resist real-life drama and tragedy? How's this for a title: 'A Hero's Story?' You know, with a question mark, since you don't know for sure. Get it? We might both get good grades yet!" Mel picked up her bag and headed for the door. "Well, guess I'll head home now and leave you to get your story worked out."

"Oh, no, you don't! If I'm going to stay up all night writing this thing, you're staying up with me! Go call your parents and tell them." As Mel headed down the hall toward the phone, Mardea shouted after her. "Hey, where can I get a pair of those funky boots?"

From the conclusion of the report, "A Hero's Story?" by Mardea Trye and Mel Zeusdatter:

"...I don't know which of those two men who died in the battle for control of the Amistad *was my ancestor. I'll probably never know. I like to think he's the one who fought to help fellow slaves become heroes for freedom. Either way, he was part of a heroic event, and because of him, I get to tell you this story. Because of him, the story of the* Amistad *is partly my story, too. I'm proud of that."*

Footnotes
1. Lester, Julius. *From Slave Ship to Freedom Road.* Dial Books for Young Readers, 1998.
2. The Spanish schooner *La Amistad* was carrying slaves from Sierra Leone to Cuba in 1839. The captives mutinied and took over the ship, which was later captured by American troops off the east coast of the United States. The Africans were jailed, while their legal status was debated in the courts. Ultimately, the U.S. Supreme Court freed them in a ground-breaking decision that became a symbol of the abolitionist movement.
3. Harpies were ugly, ill-tempered monsters, half bird and half woman, whom the gods used to torment their enemies. They were famous for their piercing shrieks and their tendency to steal anything that caught their fancy.
4. From *From Slave Ship to Freedom Road* by Julius Lester. Text copyright © 1998 by Julius Lester. Used by permission of Dial Books for Young Readers, a division of Penguin Group

(USA) LLC.

5. The nine Muses were the product of a nine-day affair between Zeus and Mnemosyne. Almost a year later, the sisters were born on nine consecutive days. So birth order didn't have quite the meaning it does in human families.

6. Ares was the son of Zeus and Hera, Zeus' third wife, so he was half-brother to the Muses. While renowned as a god of war, Ares proved himself to be a cowardly, immoral brute.

CHAPTER 7
URANIA'S MISSION: WRITTEN IN THE STARS

Urania, there's a young man in India who could benefit from your gifts as Muse of the sciences of the heavens. He shares his father's dedication to astronomy, but scorns his mother's belief in astrology with youthful arrogance. While encouraging his interest in astronomy, you will help him learn to appreciate astrology as a time-honored, if less objective, view of people's relationship to the cosmos, and to respect tradition and those who embrace it.

Bangalore, India

"Alim, is that you? Come to the sunroom. There's mail for you."

Alim broke into a trot as he entered the house and heard his mother's words. *Is it here? The letter I've been waiting for?*

"Amma, is it from ISRO? Is it the application?"

"I believe it is. But please stop and give your mother a kiss, before you get so excited you forget me entirely!" Alim's mother and older sister Anandita were huddled at the table, as they always seemed to be these days, deep into planning the details of Anandita's upcoming wedding. Alim planted a quick kiss on his mother's cheek and grabbed the envelope. He forced himself to open it carefully, so as not to tear the precious contents.

"Yes! It's the invitation to apply! This means I have a chance to get into the summer program. Now I need to decide on the perfect project to propose. I just **have** to get in!"

"I'm sure you will come up with a wonderful project, and they would be lucky to have you. But don't forget, my brilliant boy, that there is sometimes wisdom in things that don't go according to our wishes, as well. Either it's in the stars, or it's not."

"Oh, Amma, enough with the stars! You know I don't believe in that nonsense! The stars don't have anything to do with it. If my paper is good enough, I'll get in. And I **have** to get in this year!"

"Don't be so sure," countered Amma with a small smile. "The stars have served us well in the past. You thought you'd die if you didn't get in last year, and look what happened! The Director left and the program fell apart. If you'd gotten in, you'd have lost your chance at the experience you really want."

"And what about my 'lucky stars?'" Alim's sister looked up from the catalog of flowers she was studying, to challenge him. "A year ago I thought I would marry Mitra and be blissful forever. If Amma hadn't made me compare our natal charts, I could have made a terrible mistake! I might never have looked twice at Sabari, and then I wouldn't be planning to marry the perfect man for me and be the happiest bride in all of India!"

"Lucky stars, BAH! If it makes you two happy to fuss over star charts and planetary alignments, go ahead and waste your time. But I'm a scientist and I know it's just silly superstition. I'm going to my room to work on my application."

"Oh, Alim, there's a new girl here to help Lavina with the cooking and cleaning. Remember I told you that Vaani has to help her mother in Delhi for a few weeks? She recommended this girl—her name is Rani—to fill in for her. She'll be taking care of your room, so be courteous to her."

"I will, Amma. But I'm going to be very busy working on my paper. I hope she won't be loud or clumsy."

"It's only for a short time. I'm sure you'll hardly notice her."

Alim was busy at his computer when Urania tapped on his door.

"What?" he asked.

"May I come in? I'm the new housemaid. I need to gather your laundry."

"Come."

Rani entered and moved toward Alim. "I'm Rani. I'll be helping Lavina for a while."

Alim grudgingly glanced up from the computer screen at this girl who addressed him so boldly. He was surprised at what he saw. Rani didn't look Indian at all. She was tall—taller than Alim—and sturdily built. She seemed to be older than his twelve years but younger than Anandita's nineteen. She had very fair skin, dark brown hair held back by a headband decorated with stars, and eyes of a strange violet shade. Alim realized that he was staring and looked away. "OK. But don't interrupt me. I'm working on a very important project."

"Lavina told me. She says you're applying for a special program at the Indian Space Research Organization, where your father works. I'd like to hear what you're working on. I know a little about space and the stars, myself."

"Right," snapped Alim scornfully. "You're probably busy planning your life according to the position of the stars, like my mother and sister. That's all foolishness, you know."

"Is it? Well, I'd certainly never want to argue with a scientist like yourself!" Rani didn't know whether to be amused or annoyed at the boy's arrogance. But he didn't seem to notice her sarcasm. In fact, he barely noticed her at all! And she had been warned. Besides, she'd met plenty of arrogant young men at home. *Maybe a little flattery will get his attention. I don't know how I'll influence him, if I can't make him see me as anything more than the invisible "help."*

"Lavina said you have to write a paper on astronomy. She's sure you'll get in, because you're so smart. Have you decided on your subject?"

"It's a proposal for a summer research project. And no, not yet. I have two ideas." Alim's eyes lit up at the chance to talk about it, even if it was only to a housemaid. "I'm thinking about either the new 'Goldilocks' planets [1] they're discovering or new findings about supermassive black holes." He glanced back at Rani and shook his head. "But I'm sure that doesn't mean anything to you."

"Actually, it does. I told you, I know about astronomy. There's even a planet named after me," Urania announced cheerfully [2]. "Did you know some modern astrologers take the gravitational pull and electromagnetic influence of supermassive black holes into account in their work? They find that they can make more accurate predictions that way."

Alim swung around on his swivel chair to face her, stunned to hear this coming from a lowly housemaid. Recovering, he scoffed. "Hah! It figures that those phonies would latch onto anything to make them sound smart, and make their competitors look bad in the bargain. Maybe you should stick to your daily horoscope and leave real science to people who understand the difference! Wait, what did you say about a planet named after you?"

"Yes. My name is really Urania, like the planet Uranus."

"So you mean you were named after the planet?"

"Um, right," Rani mumbled, embarrassed to be caught in such a thoughtless slip.

Alim shrugged his shoulders. "I have to get back to work. My laundry is over there." He nodded toward the corner and turned back to the computer, puzzled but dismissive.

Rani resisted the urge to lash out at Alim's smugness and instead busied herself gathering laundry and straightening the room, while Alim scanned a series of websites. When he left to take a phone call, Rani went to the computer. *I know he'll at least see what's here. What can I find that might impress him? Ah, maybe this....* She brought up a site about famous scientists, like Johannes Kepler, Carl Jung, and Louis Pasteur, who argued in defense of astrology, and quickly left the room.

Alim returned to his computer, having put the odd conversation with Rani out of his mind. *What's this? How did this get here? Strange!* Alim read a little before losing interest and returning to his research.

The next day at school, Alim had trouble keeping his mind on his classes. April break was coming up and he needed to decide on his project before then so he could spend the week working on his paper. Ideas swirled in his head. *Goldilocks planets are interesting, but trendy. Supermassive blacks are more cutting edge and theoretical. Maybe that would impress them more.* He debated with himself all the way home on the bus, so deep in thought that he didn't even remember to look out the window, as he usually did, at the frangipani and cannon ball trees as the bus passed Lalbagh Gardens. By the time he got home, he had decided to choose based on which topic had the strongest online sources. He grabbed a parotha [3] from the kitchen and trotted toward his room. Amma and Anandita were in their usual places in the sunroom, this time arguing about the menu for the wedding dinner. He tiptoed past the doorway, to avoid their attention and get straight to work.

In his room he found a handwritten note. He read, "I saw this in a magazine. I hope you don't mind my boldness, but I found it interesting and thought you might, too." It was signed "Rani." *What? Who's Rani?* It took a minute for Alim to remember the new maid he'd met the day before. *The housemaid wrote me a note?* It made no sense. She was a girl, a housemaid, and not even their permanent help! Who did she think she was, writing him a note and recommending reading to him? Looking at the article she had left for him, his irritation changed to surprise. It was about a new study, suggesting that supermassive black holes grow by feeding on binary star partners. He was fascinated, in spite of himself.

Rani felt nervous as she knocked on Alim's door. She heard the same brusque "Come" as the day before, and entered. A small smile crossed her lips, when she saw Alim deeply engrossed in the article.

Alim looked up. "You're Rani, right? Did you leave this for me?"

Rani nodded.

"Why? Who showed you this?"

"I hope you're not angry. I didn't mean to presume. But I thought it might help you decide on your project. It's interesting, don't you think?"

"You read this? You understood it? How do you know about this stuff?"

"I've studied both astronomy and astrology a lot. Where I come from, I'm sort of an expert." She wanted to say more, to impress him with her knowledge. But she knew she had to move slowly, if she wanted him to take her seriously.

Still wary, but getting used to outrageous pronouncements from this totally unconventional housemaid, Alim responded with a blend of fascination and disdain. "Humph. Astronomy **and** astrology? Why both? How can you know anything about real science and still study astrology?"

"Not everyone thinks they're mutually exclusive, you know. Astrology's been around a lot longer than what we call astronomy, and lots of smart people believe it helps them understand their lives and make good decisions."

"Ridiculous! Now you sound like my mother and sister."

"What's wrong with that?" She bristled a little. "You mother seems pretty smart, and I don't know when I've met anyone quite as happy as your sister."

"Why are you arguing with me? Why are you even talking to me? You're the housemaid! And not a very good one at that."

They both looked around the room. The bed was rumpled. Dust was building up on the windowsill and Rani had left a trail of dirty clothes scattered across the floor. At first, she was alarmed. *What if Alim complains to his mother? What if I lose my place here? How will I work with him?* Then she realized this might be an opportunity. If she couldn't yet dazzle him with her vast knowledge, perhaps she could disarm him with something close to honesty.

Rani laughed, breaking the tension. "You're right; I'm not a very good housemaid, am I? I really don't know anything about cleaning and cooking and all of that. Can I tell you something the others here don't know?"

"Um, I guess so."

"I'm never going to be a real housemaid. I'm doing this as

108

a favor to Vaani. She was worried about leaving your mother shorthanded while she visited her mother. She didn't want to lose her place here or to burden the rest of the staff with her duties. I volunteered to take her place, as a sort of experiment."

"Experiment? What do you mean?"

"It's confusing. But the thing is, I'm really not from a household servant kind of family. My family is quite wealthy. My sisters and I have never done any housework, to speak of. In fact, we have servants of our own to do all that for us! I'm actually a student. But I'm sort of a bookworm and my sisters tease me about it. They don't think I'm good for much besides studying. So when I heard about Vaani's situation—she's a friend of the family—I offered to fill in to show my sisters I can do other things, practical things, too, not that any of my sisters could make a bed to save her life!"

"So let me get this straight. You're here to be a housemaid, but you're not a housemaid. You're trying to prove something to a bunch of silly sisters. You're really a student who studies astronomy **and** astrology, and you think you can help me learn about them, too. Right?"

"That's about it," she replied sheepishly.

"So you brought me that article. And I'll bet you left that website about Kepler and Pasteur on my computer, too."

"Yes, I did. But I've learned that both astronomy and astrology have value. And I didn't like the way you laughed at your mother and sister."

"You didn't **like** it?" Alim was truly shocked. "You're a housemaid, at least here and now. Why should I care what you like or don't like? Sure, astrology has value—it keeps foolish women busy so they don't get in the way of serious science! I told you yesterday not to interrupt me. So go 'maid' something—you could use the practice. And **maybe** I won't tell Amma that you don't know what you're doing, though she'll figure that out soon enough, herself."

"OK, OK. I didn't mean to upset you. But can we make a deal? You show me how this bed is supposed to look, and I'll show you another great website about supermassive black holes."

Alim felt equal parts irritation at her impudence and curiosity about what she might have to show him. This whole situation was absurd! It was actually funny, in a way. He laughed, in spite of himself.

"You are unbelievable! OK, I won't say anything to Amma, at least not yet. And I'll show you how to make a bed. But that website had better be good!"

Later, as he pored over an online discussion of the effects of sound waves, coming from an SMBH [4] in the Perseus galaxy, on star growth 300,000 light years away, he had to admit it was good! So good that he didn't even balk at a theory, proposed by an astrologer, about how black holes affect conditions for people whose dominant planets are under their influence. Instead of abandoning the site, he rolled his eyes and chuckled at Rani's persistence.

In the next few days, Alim saw little of Rani. Lavina kept her busy and his room was tended before he got home. He had to give her credit; his bed was neatly made and most of the dust was gone from the windowsill. Still, each day, she had left a message for him. On Wednesday, it was a poem, written out neatly and left on his desk. It read:

> *"The game of science is, in principle, without end.*
> *He who decides one day that scientific statements*
> *do not call for further test,*
> *and that they can be regarded as finally verified,*
> *retires from the game."*
> -Karl Popper [5]

Rani had added a P.S. "Whether your scientific statement is 'astrology is science' or 'astrology isn't science,' doesn't it call for further test?"

On Thursday, he found another website waiting for him. It was a blog by an astrologer. Alim skimmed a series of arguments supporting the idea that the position and movement of heavenly bodies influence the earth and people's lives. A second entry pointed out problems in the arguments many scientists use to discredit astrology. It was, Alim had to admit, not entirely illogical in its observations.

Alim couldn't help thinking about Rani. She completely bewildered him. She was so different from the girls he knew. He loved his mother and sister, of course. But girls, in general, always seemed emotional, irrational, and silly. Now here was Rani, who had no business being there as a housemaid. *She doesn't know anything about the things girls are supposed to know, but she seems to know almost as much about astronomy as I do!* And not only was she not afraid to interfere in his business, she was actively trying to influence his thinking! He wanted to dismiss her as just another female who made no sense, but somehow he couldn't. He needed to talk to his father. That night after dinner, Alim joined Mr. Lingam on the patio, where he had gone for a smoke.

"Hi, Baba. How was work today?"

"Ah, Alim. Come sit with me. Work is work. I love my job, but right now we're analyzing a huge collection of data and it can get rather boring. That's never been my favorite part of research. How about you? Have you decided yet about your summer program proposal?"

"I think so. I want to study supermassive black holes—maybe combine a literature review with exploring ways to monitor the effects of our galaxy's SMBH on telecommunication and weather satellites. Black holes are amazing! They explain so much about how galaxies form and how things work around them."

"That sounds excellent! I think you have a good chance of getting into the program. But do your best on the proposal and I'll be proud of you whether you're chosen or not."

Alim fished the poem Rani had left him out of his pocket and handed it to his father. "Have you seen this before, Baba? What do you think it means?"

Mr. Lingam read the poem. He raised his eyebrows.

"I know Popper's work, but I don't think I've seen this before. I like it. Where did you find this?"

Alim was embarrassed about his strange conversations with Rani and the fact that he was challenged and confused by them. He hesitated, but ended up telling his father the story.

"So, our young fill-in maid is also a scientist? And she's defending astrology to you? Did she write the question at the end of the poem, then?"

Alim nodded.

"This is quite remarkable!" Baba continued with a twinkle in his eyes. "I may have to come home early one of these days to meet this unusual young woman. Your conversations remind me of some I had myself, when I was a few years older than you."

"What conversations? Did someone try to convince you that astrology is more than superstition?"

"You could say that. But I don't believe I was ever so sure as you seem to be that it isn't."

"Baba, **you** don't believe in astrology, do you? How can you, and still be a scientist?"

"I'm not convinced that astrology is a scientifically valid way to predict events and make choices. I don't consult my chart before making decisions. But some of my colleagues do, and quite a few good scientists have believed in or defended astrology—Galileo, Newton, Kepler...."

"I know. Rani left a website up on my computer about them. But how **could** they believe all that?"

"Maybe they were trying to be true to the spirit of science, as they understood it. Think about it—there are many things we used to believe that science has disproved, and many things we believe now that scientists thought were impossible, or nonsense, in earlier times. The fact that we can't explain something doesn't make it false, and scientists can't let prejudice rule our thinking. After all, science moves forward by revising and adapting its beliefs, not insisting on them." Baba warmed to his topic. "I think that's what Popper is trying to say—that real scientists can't just dismiss something without testing it out, or assume that what we believe now will always hold true. That would be as unscientific as clinging to a belief simply because it's customary or appealing, without proof. People have believed in astrology for a long time and it seems to help some people make good choices and live their lives well. Why be so quick to criticize it, before you've even done your homework?"

"You just say that because Amma and Anandita believe in it. Anandita is sure that Amma saved her from a bad marriage by making her use her star chart. But she can't be sure that she'll be happy forever with Sabari, or that she wouldn't have been happy with Mitra."

"I agree that there are no guarantees. And you're right; your mother's enthusiasm has made me look at it differently. Did you know that your mother wouldn't agree to marry me until we compared our charts? And look how well that's turned out! Your Amma isn't a scientist, but she's a very smart, wise woman, and I'm not eager to criticize anything that helped me win her heart! So you see, Alim, sometimes even a scientist has to keep an open mind about things that don't seem clear and logical—maybe a scientist more than anyone! I'll tell you something few people know, if you promise not to spread it around."

Alim nodded.

"The new Director at ISRO told me one day, over tea, that he had another job offer when our agency contacted him about taking over. Both were very good opportunities for him. When he had trouble deciding, he consulted an astrologer for advice. He chose ISRO and we're lucky to have him."

"**What**? Dr. Bannarji believes in astrology? The one who will read my proposal and decide if I make it into the summer program?"

"Yes, Dr. Bannarji. And maybe not religiously, but he thought it had value as a tool to help him decide."

Alim went to bed with a head full of new thoughts and questions.

Meanwhile, Rani was facing her own challenges. Lavina noticed that she was waiting to tend Alim's room until he was home and told her to take care of it earlier in the day.

"Alim has important work to do. You shouldn't interrupt him."

Rani had to obey, but it limited her ability to complete her mission. She had managed to leave him a message each day, but she knew that wouldn't be enough. She had to find a way to spend more time with him. She pondered this, as she dusted in the sunroom. Mrs. Lingam and Anandita sat on cushioned chairs, arguing about what dessert to serve at the wedding dinner.

Mrs. Lingam said, "You can't go wrong with a lovely, warm gajar halva [6]. It's traditional, and nice after a spicy meal."

"But Amma, the weather will be so hot! We need something light to cool the palate."

"How about ice cream or, better yet, sherbet?"

The word *sherbet* startled Rani, with its close kinship to *sorbet*, and filled her with an almost painful yearning for the delicacy at stake in the Muses' missions. She tuned into the conversation.

"Sherbet is nice, but everyone serves it. I've had blood orange sherbet at two dinners this month alone. I want something unusual!"

Without thinking, Rani jumped in. "What about pear sorbet? Where I come from, it's a great delicacy. There's nothing better after a spicy meal, and pear is the perfect fruit!" She realized immediately that she had overstepped. She lowered her head and mumbled an apology, as the two women stared at her. Clearly, they were shocked to hear her enter their conversation. But then they exchanged looks of excitement.

"It's perfect!" said Anandita. "Sherbet is common, but not sorbet, and pears aren't grown here. So this would be quite exotic. What a wonderful idea!"

"Yes! It sounds just right. Would Lavina know how to make it? Or do you know how, Rani?"

"Oh, no. I wouldn't dare!" replied Rani, looking down at her shoes. "Lavina is a good cook. I'm sure she could find a recipe and make it."

"Well, thank you, Rani! I'll talk to her about it. Perhaps you could be her official taster, since you're familiar with it."

Rani's eyes widened in alarm. "Oh, no! It doesn't matter what I think. Anandita should taste it. She's the bride—it has to please her! I think I'm needed in the laundry now."

Rani rushed out of the room. *How foolish of me! I nearly got myself in trouble that time! But would tasting it really count? After all, it wouldn't be Athena's pear sorbet. Maybe just a taste as part of fitting in and completing my mission….*

Rani knew she needed to talk to Alim. That evening she offered to stay and straighten up the kitchen, so Lavina could leave early. She took her time. *Not bad at all,* she thought, giving the counter a final swipe with the dishrag. As the sky darkened, she saw Alim head outside with his telescope. She followed him.

"Alim! Are you going somewhere?"

"Oh, you startled me! Up on the roof. It's never very dark in the city, but there's no moon tonight. I might have a good view of Sagittarius. It's the constellation that contains the Milky Way's SMBH, Sagittarius A-Star."

"Is that why you want to see it? Not because Sagittarius is your sun sign?" Rani teased.

"Don't start. Of course that's why. You know I don't believe in that stuff." But, Rani noticed, he said it with less disdain than before.

"May I look? Would you mind?"

"I guess not. Come on up." What would have been unthinkable with an ordinary housemaid somehow seemed natural with Rani.

They sat on the roof, enjoying the slight breeze freshening the warm, humid air. The sky was clear. Alim set up his telescope and found Sagittarius. He motioned for Rani to take a turn.

"Look!" Rani nudged Alim. I think I see Messier 55. See? Did you know that it's over 17,000 light years away?"

"Let me see. Where?"

Rani showed Alim the star cluster.

"I think you're right. I can't believe you know that! Look, I see the Pistol Star, too."

The two explored the constellation enthusiastically for some time, before sitting down to relax on the roof.

"Beautiful, isn't it?" Rani asked. "Let's see, Sagittarius: the Archer. Direct and honest, unemotional but intuitive. Intellectual, curious, philosophical, energetic, but also impulsive. Does that sound like you?"

"Parts of that sound like anyone who might hear it."

"You have a point. But astrology isn't just about your sun sign. Lots of things go into figuring out what it has to tell you. What if I told you that the stars are telling me, right now, that you're going to be a famous scientist someday?" [7]

"I'd say you have a great imagination! I have enough trouble believing that some stars, 17,000 light years away, can define me or control my life! And now you say you can tell my future, without even looking at my chart? Ha! Where's the proof?"

"There's not much solid proof, but there's a lot of evidence that's hard to dismiss. And there's no disproof. We know that the moon causes ocean tides. Mental patients get jumpy during sunspot activity. Oysters open their shells in response to the moon's position. Why is it so hard to accept that stars and planets might influence people in other ways?"

"I guess it's not so hard to accept that they **might**, just that they **do**, without proof."

"Fair enough. But you're a scientist. Why not figure out a way to test it? To show scientifically that astrology either does or doesn't 'work' in predicting things for people?"

"I'm sure scientists have done that before."

"Yes, but they've never been able to truly prove or disprove it. Maybe you could."

"I'm going to be a little busy, working on supermassive black holes!"

"So you've decided? It's a good choice. I'm sure your project will be excellent. You really are as smart as Lavina said. But here's something to think about—remember I told you some astrologers are adjusting their predictions to account for the effects of SMBHs? Maybe you could work a way to test their results into your project, along with your main study. It would be interesting and unexpected, so it could make your proposal stand out from the rest."

"Or they might see it and not take me seriously at all!" But as he said this, Alim was remembering what his father told him about Dr. Bannarji.

"Well, we wouldn't want that. Just don't be so hard on your mom and sister, OK? They may be smarter than you

116

think. By the way, I clipped this from today's paper. Thought it might interest you." Rani handed Alim a small slip of paper. "I should go. Thanks for letting me look at Sagittarius with you. Good night!"

"Good night," Alim answered, puzzled, as always, by Rani's fearless, unconventional behavior. He unfolded the paper. He groaned. It was part of the horoscope column, the message for Sagittarians. It read, "The coming weeks hold great promise for new opportunities. Be alert. If you don't let pride cloud your judgment, you are sure to succeed."

Alim snorted. But he stayed on the roof, watching the stars and thinking, for a long time.

The next morning Alim watched for a chance to talk to his mother, alone.

"Amma, when I was born, did you have my natal chart drawn, like you did for Anandita?"

"Of course. Why do you ask?"

"Just curious. Could I see it?"

"Certainly. But why now? You've never been interested, before."

"It's just something I've been thinking about. Amma, did you know that Dr. Bannarji took the job at ISRO partly because an astrologer told him to?"

"I did know that. Your father told me. What's this all about, Alim?"

"I've been thinking about including a survey about astrologers who consider supermassive black holes in their readings as an 'extra' in my project proposal. It might catch Dr. Bannarji's attention, that's all."

Mrs. Lingam raised an eyebrow. "What a fascinating idea! How will seeing your chart help?"

"I just thought it would help me understand how astrologers work, so I can plan the survey better. Not that I believe in it or anything, but it might make my project stand out from the others. And maybe I'll disprove it once and for all!"

"Well, I think it's a wonderful idea," Amma said, smiling. "I'll get your chart right away."

As the April school break came to a close, Alim put the final touches on his proposal. He was satisfied. *I did my best,* he thought. *I think it's good enough to get me in.* He wanted, more than ever, to be chosen for the program. Not just for the pride and honor of it, but because he was excited about this project—all of it! He couldn't wait to study the literature and test his hypothesis about SMBHs. But he also looked forward to the astrology survey. Including it was risky, but he felt confident, based on his inside knowledge about Dr. Bannarji. *At least, after this, they won't be able to accuse me of rejecting astrology out of prejudice!*

Alim found himself wanting to show Rani his finished proposal. She could be annoying and pushy, and her interference was totally inappropriate. But he wasn't allowed to show his work to his father, so as to avoid concerns about an unfair advantage. Rani was the only person he could think of who might understand and appreciate it. He went looking for her.

Meanwhile, in the kitchen, Lavina was testing a recipe for pear sorbet. She called across the room to Rani, who was polishing silver. "Come taste this for me, Rani. Mrs. Lingam says you're the expert on this dessert, and as nervous as Anandita is these days, I don't want to ask her until I know it's good."

Rani looked up, startled. *Do I dare? Would Mother find out? What would she think? Would I ruin it for everyone, even though it's not Athena's recipe?*

"Um, I really don't think that's a good idea. I have a cold today and I don't think I could judge it fairly." Just then, her cell phone rang. She picked it up, grateful for the interruption, but puzzled. She'd gotten the phone so she could be available to Lavina anytime, but she'd given the number to no one else— who else would use it? "Hello?"

Her sister Terpsichore's voice was clear and insistent. "Meet me by the umbrella tree in the yard—**now**!" The phone went silent.

"Sorry, Lavina, I have to run this laundry out to the line right now. I don't want it to dry wrinkled." She dashed out the door with the basket before Lavina could reply.

Terpsichore waited on the far side of the tree, breathless. "What's going on?" she asked, before Rani could ask her the same question. "Mother yanked me away from my mission and sent me here with a message, and no explanation. 'Tell your sister Urania **no**! Athena's recipe or not, it would be unfair to the others and violate the spirit of this whole plan, for you to taste even one bite.' Rani, what **is** she talking about? You weren't trying to sneak some pear sorbet, were you?"

"No, of course not! But I almost had to taste some, whether I wanted to or not." Rani explained. "Your call saved me, though I don't know what I'm going to do when I go back in." Terpsichore began to laugh; Rani joined her. It was absurd! "I can't believe Mother knew that! At least now we know there's no room for bending the rules, even a little!"

When the giggles subsided, Terpsichore asked, "Since I'm here, how's your mission going? Anything I can help with?"

"A few days ago, I would have welcomed ideas on how to cut through this boy's stubborn smugness. But he's coming around nicely, now. I think I'll be OK—that is, unless you know how to wash windows without leaving streaks!"

"Windows? What are you talking about?"

"Never mind—too complicated!"

"Then I guess I'll be off. See you soon, back at home."

Alim saw Rani through the window, talking to a girl about her age. He charged out the door, just as the other girl disappeared around the side of the house.

"Hi, Rani. I was looking for you. Who was that?"

"Just my sister," Rani answered, glad not to have to concoct a story when the truth would do. "She had a message from our mother. Something about saving my appetite for dessert at home later." Rani stifled a leftover giggle as she heard herself say the words. "Did I forget to dust your room?"

"No." Alim suddenly felt awkward. "It's just that I finished my proposal for ISRO. I thought you might want to see it. You know, since you were so interested and all."

"I'd love to see it! Let me hang this laundry, and I'll come right in. OK?"

"OK."

Whew! Saved! Lavina won't argue with a summons from Alim.

Alim's paper was even better than Rani had expected. She told him she was sure he'd be selected, based on this work. The astrology survey pleased her, though its design still suggested heavy skepticism. She looked up from the document and saw Alim's star chart on his desk.

"What's this?" she asked.

"It's the chart my mom had done when I was born. I used it to learn about astrology, so I'd know how to ask the questions on the survey."

"Do you know how to read this?"

"Not very well, but I understand some things. I still can't imagine it could tell me anything useful."

"Well, let's see. When's your proposal due?"

"No later than Wednesday. I thought I'd send it with Baba early next week."

"What if we look at your chart together? It might tell us which day would be best—most favorable, you know."

"Seriously? You expect me to let this thing tell me when to apply? That's ridiculous!"

Rani shrugged. "Up to you. I should get back to work."

"Wait a minute. Would you show me? I guess it couldn't hurt."

Four months later, at a reception honoring ISRO's summer students at the close of the program, Dr. Bannarji sought out Alim.

"Young Master Lingam! A worthy son to follow in his father's footsteps! You should be proud of your work this summer. Your project was a great success and, I hope, only the beginning of your studies in this area. Though I must admit, I wish your astrology survey had produced more conclusive results."

"Thank you, Dr. B! Me, too. I guess it's up to some other scientist to determine whether astrology is science or superstition. I think I'll stick to astronomical research—it suits me better."

"And I hope we'll be able to work with you as you do that. Speaking of working together, there's something I want to talk to you about. You know that ISRO is starting an outreach program for elementary students—an astronomy club that will meet monthly during the school year. The staff here is so impressed with your work that we'd like you to be one of three youth volunteers working with that program. We can't pay you, but we can offer you access to our labs and equipment so you can continue your research, and I think you could learn a lot as you help the children learn. Are you interested?"

Alim's eyes flashed with excitement and mischief. "I don't know, Dr. B. I'll have to consult my chart first, to see if it's written in the stars!"

Footnotes

1. A Goldilocks planet is a planet that lies within the habitable zone of its star—not too close, but not too far away, suggesting that it could have liquid water and sustain life.
2. Actually, the planet is named for Uranus, Greek god of the sky and Urania's grandfather. But a girl can dream, right?
3. A *parotha* is a flaky flatbread, a standard in South Indian cuisine.
4. SMBH is short for supermassive black holes.
5. From *The Logic of Scientific Discovery* by Karl Popper. Original English text copyright © 1959 by Karl Popper. Used by permission of the Karl Popper Copyright Office.
6. *Gajar halva* is a carrot pudding, spiced with cardamom.
7. One of Urania's gifts, as Muse of the sciences of the heavens, is the ability to read the future in the stars. So she's not kidding!

CHAPTER 8
CLIO'S MISSION: OLD FOOLS AND MAMA'S BOYS

Clio, Muse of History, a young man in China needs your help. He's in trouble for showing disrespect for the history of his people. Yet he has unusual gifts that lend themselves to bringing history alive for his peers. Your task is to help him recognize the importance of history and connect it with his passion and talents.

Shanghai, The People's Republic of China
For the first time in his twelve years, Kun had gotten in trouble at school. He hung his head as he handed his father a note from his teacher. His father took it with raised eyebrows and read aloud:

Dear Kun's father,
I must bring to your attention a troubling event. Kun has always been a good boy, apart from his tendency to doodle on his papers during class. So you can imagine my surprise when

I heard him after history class making fun of General Yue Fei [1], calling him a "foolish old mama's boy." I knew you would want to know that your son needs help learning to respect our great heroes of the past. I'll leave you to deal with it as you see fit. Because of Kun's good behavior until now, there will be no further consequences at school unless problems persist.

Sincerely,
Teacher Yang

"Is this true, Kun?

The boy nodded silently.

"Why would you say such a thing? How could you be so disrespectful?"

"I'm sorry, Baba. I just get so bored when Teacher Yang goes on and on about these ancient people, and wars a million years ago! This emperor, and that dynasty, and who came after whom…. Boring! It's nice outside, and I'm cooped up listening to stories about some general who couldn't even go to war without his mother's permission! What's brave about that? So I made a joke. That's all."

Kun noticed the spark of anger in his father's eyes and prepared for the worst.

"You laugh at Yue Fei's courage and victories? You're just an ignorant boy! How do you dare judge our ancestral heroes?" In the silence that followed, Kun rubbed the toe of his shoe on the carpet, while his father struggled to calm himself. Father sighed.

"Oh, Kun, I'm disappointed in you. Maybe I haven't done all I should to teach you proper respect. Your behavior shows disregard for both our national heroes and for mothers, not to mention your teacher. Maybe being without a mother for so long has been worse for you than I realized."

"No, Baba! I don't mind being just the two of us. Mama died so long ago I hardly even remember her. We're a team. I don't need a mother."

"We do well together, it's true. But no child should be without a mother, and it's obvious you haven't learned to honor mothers or a son's duty to his mother. We need to do something about that. Now go do your homework while I think

123

about it."

The next evening, dinner was silent, disturbed only by the frequent rumble of planes coming or going from Hongqiao International Airport. Finally, Baba set down his chopsticks and leaned back in his chair. He cleared his throat. Kun recognized the signs of a pronouncement coming and sat perfectly still, nervously awaiting his fate.

"Kun, I've thought long and hard about your behavior at school. I came up with an idea. Today I made some calls and arranged what I think will be a good experience for you. I hope it will help you learn proper respect." He paused and looked Kun directly in the eyes, with an intensity that told the boy to take his words seriously.

"What experience, Baba?"

"Every day, on the way home from school, you ride your bike past the Yixian Home for the Elderly. Starting next week, you won't just ride by. Two days a week, you'll stop and spend two hours as a volunteer. The staff there will assign you a resident to visit. I've asked them to choose women who are mothers. You will talk to them, read to them, write letters for them, take walks, play games, or whatever they want to do."

"But, Baba! I don't know any of those people, and they're all so **old**! What can we possibly talk about?"

Baba held up his hand against the interruption. "You'll encourage them to talk about themselves—about the past, their families, careers, ancestors, or history. You will listen. Above all, you will show the utmost respect. I hope this will help you appreciate the value of age, experience, tradition, and family duty. Yes, 'those people' are old, though not nearly as ancient as General Yue Fei! But that's exactly why they have much to teach you."

"Baba, please," Kun begged. "I promise I'll be respectful! I promise I'll pay attention in history class and not make fun. I promise!"

"It's arranged. It's done. You'll begin on Monday."

"How long do I have to do this?"

"We'll start with a month and see what happens."

"A month? That's eight times!"

124

"Well, I'm glad to see that you pay more attention in math class than in history," Baba replied, half-smiling. "Now please clean up the table and do your homework."

Monday afternoon, Kun parked his bike and trudged slowly toward the entrance to Yixian Home for the Elderly, feeling heavier with every step. He pushed open the door and approached the reception desk inside. Two women sat at the desk. One seemed quite old, with white hair and a slight frown. The other was surprisingly young, maybe in her twenties. Even more surprising was that she had dark red hair, rolled up on her head in a complicated, mysterious fashion, and deep purple eyes like none he'd seen before. She wore a long, belted dress that matched her eyes. She stood and greeted him with a smile.

"Are you Kun? I'm Clio. I've been expecting you. I just started working with the volunteer program here. I talked to your father on the phone and I'll be supervising your time here." As Kun bowed his greeting, she held out her hand to him. He overcame his surprise and gave it a quick, weak shake.

"This is Cheng Shu. She knows everything that goes on around here, so if you need anything, ask her," Clio explained. Kun held out his hand uncertainly and was both relieved and flustered when the woman bowed her greeting. *I'm already messing up and I haven't even met a resident yet,* he thought.

"Come with me," Clio said. "Since I'm new here myself and I've just met you, I wasn't sure how to choose a resident for you right away. So I thought, for today, we could join some people in the library. It's a group that gets together weekly to tell each other stories. You can meet some of the residents and we'll see how it goes. They choose different kinds of stories each week. Today, it's something from their past— anything that happened to them before they moved in here. Sound good?"

Sounds like torture, Kun thought to himself. Out loud, he said, "Sure. Sounds good."

When they reached the library, a man who looked older than anyone Kun had ever seen was finishing a story. Polite applause startled awake two others who had nodded off. Clio introduced Kun and had the residents introduce themselves to him. He bowed dutifully and took a seat next to Clio.

"Who's next?" invited a man about Kun's father's age, who seemed to be in charge.

A small woman who was surprisingly pretty (*Can someone that old be pretty?*) raised her hand timidly. The leader nodded in her direction and she began to speak in a soft, sweet voice about visiting her grandson, who was now a grown man, when he was a baby. It was hard to hear her, and what he could hear made him long to bolt, jump on his bike, and do something—anything!—interesting with the afternoon. She went on and on in that sweet, gushy way his own Nai-Nai [2] acted when he and his father visited her. *And I have to listen to this for two hours?* Kun thought. *Just for making a joke about some ancient general? Not fair!*

Kun was startled out of his thoughts about the injustice of it all by a change of speakers. This new voice was loud and a bit gruff; it commanded attention. Kun jerked in his chair and looked around. The speaker was a rather round woman in a wheelchair. Her graying hair was cut short, and bright red lipstick contrasted startlingly with her pale skin. She launched into a story about her son and nephew, who had taken positions on opposite sides of the Cultural Revolution of the 1960s. Unlike the previous speaker, this woman was a born storyteller. Her eyes flashed. She used different voices for the people in the story and made dramatic gestures with her hands and arms—something Kun rarely saw except in foreigners. He was swept up in the story. Barely realizing what he was doing, he grabbed some napkins from a nearby table, pulled a pen from his pocket, and began to sketch the pictures her words put in his mind.

Clio noticed the change in Kun's manner and watched closely as his fingers created cartoon drawings, while his eyes hardly left the speaker. *What do you know? The boy's an artist! That must be the talent Mother mentioned. Now, how can I use that? Hmm... The first step—more time with this woman!*

The storyteller, Zhao Yubi, spoke for a full twenty

minutes. Not one listener nodded off. She owned the room; she certainly owned Kun's attention. When she finally ended her story with a flourish of pride, Kun looked disappointed. He tucked the napkins in his pocket.

No one wanted to follow her performance and the hour was nearly up. The group dispersed; some on foot, some in wheelchairs. Clio wasted no time.

"Zhao Yubi, may my young friend and I help you back to your room? There's something I'd like to discuss with you."

The woman looked Clio and Kun over, taking their measure.

"Come along, then. But I don't need help. I can get around fine by myself."

Zhao Yubi's room was nothing like Kun expected. It was a riot of color, with bold printed cloths over every flat surface and vivid paintings of soldiers and Chinese landmarks on every wall.

How can she sleep in here? Kun wondered. *This room would give me nightmares, if I could get to sleep at all!* But it was strangely exciting, just like its occupant.

"Here we are," Zhao Yubi remarked. "What's on your mind?"

Clio introduced herself and Kun again. Sparing no detail, she told the woman why Kun had come to Yixian Home and what was expected of him. Kun blushed, embarrassed and irked that Clio would recount his misdeeds so directly.

"Your story was wonderful and I'm sure Kun thought so, too. Would you be willing to spend some time with him? Talk, read, play games, whatever you like? I think you might get along well. I'm sure Kun could learn a lot from you."

Zhao Yubi took Kun's measure again, making him wish he'd combed his jet black hair on the way into the building. She chuckled softly.

"So, what exactly did you say about General Yue Fei, boy?"

Kun told her, his blush deepening.

Again, she chuckled.

"Disrespectful? Yes. But you remind me a little of my son at your age. In fact, you remind me a little of myself at your age! Restless, bored, and so sure that the world revolves around your feelings and interests. I could use a new challenge. Yes! I'll take on young Kun. But know this, boy, I'll send you packing at the first trace of disrespect! Understand?"

Kun, a little intimidated, mumbled, "Yes, Zhao Nai-Nai."

"Good!" Clio chirped. "Then I'll leave you to it. Kun has about an hour before he leaves for the day. Enjoy yourselves. Kun, come and find me before you go."

She moved toward the door. Kun shot her a desperate look. She took pity on him.

"Kun, why don't you start by showing Zhao Yubi the sketches you made of her story?"

The old woman's eyes lit up.

"You drew my story?"

"Um, I just doodled while you talked. I do that a lot. It helps me listen."

"Well, boy, let me see them!"

Kun fished the napkins out of his pocket as Clio left the room.

Zhao Yubi praised his drawings, but bluntly corrected details she thought were wrong. Kun, in turn, reworked the sketches on paper she supplied. Kun asked her to tell him more about her son. She startled him with direct questions about what it was like for him to live without a mother. He asked about her wheelchair.

"Don't you worry about me, boy. Just try to keep up!"

When he finally thought to look at the clock, it was fifteen minutes past his time. He had to hurry to check out with Clio and make it home for dinner.

On Thursday, the next day he was scheduled to visit the nursing home, Kun was apprehensive. His visit with Zhao Yubi had been OK, even interesting. After talking to her, he'd done an online search about the Cultural Revolution and he wanted to ask her about what he'd read. But what if Clio sent him to someone else this time? Or what if he and Zhao Yubi couldn't find anything besides the Cultural Revolution to talk about? He checked in with Clio, who sent him to Zhao Yubi's room. She was waiting for him. Her eyes were bright, but she looked somehow smaller than Kun remembered.

"I thought you might not come," she told him, straightening in her chair. "I thought I might have scared you away. I sometimes have that effect on people."

"Not me. I mean, I wasn't scared. I read about the Cultural Revolution. I want to ask you about it. And I made some more pictures. Will you look at them? And maybe tell me another story?"

When Clio peeked in the partly-open door to check on them, the two sat, head to head, examining and discussing Kun's sketches with intense concentration. *I don't know what he's learning,* she thought, *but they're certainly getting along. That's a start. If anyone here can get Kun interested in history, it's Zhao Yubi. And this might be good for her too. Kun hasn't seen how listless she is when she's not sharing her stories.*

The next Monday, Kun found Clio in Zhao Yubi's room, helping her settle into her wheelchair. The old woman looked breathless and irritable; her hands trembled.

"I'm barely ready for you, boy. Clio, here, isn't very good at this sort of thing. I called for her fifteen minutes ago. After all, I can't lie in bed all day, when I have company coming!"

Clio looked irritated in return, but managed to sound cheerful as she asked, "Zhao Yubi, before you two get lost in stories and drawings today, is there anything else Kun might do for you? Take you for a stroll outside? Write a letter for you?"

Zhao Yubi's face softened.

"Well, there is one thing. Since you've been visiting me, Kun, I've been thinking a lot about my son, Liang. He can't visit me often, since he lives in Chengdu and he has so many important responsibilities." She sighed and seemed to shrink. "I used to write to him often, but my writing has gotten so poor I can barely read it myself. He wants me to e-mail, but I can't stand computers! I'm too old for that nonsense. Kun, you could write to him for me, and maybe send one of your pictures."

Kun was startled. Zhao Yubi was so interesting and so animated during their visits that he had almost forgotten how old she was. Accustomed as he was to her energetic storytelling gestures, he hadn't noticed her trembling hands before today. He realized that he didn't want her to be weak, didn't want her to need help. But he could hardly refuse. After all, that's why he was at the nursing home in the first place. So he gathered the paper and pen she directed him to and began to write as she dictated.

Zhao Yubi's words to her son were full of praise and pride for his accomplishments and reassurance that she was well, busy, and happy. She had Kun write about their time together, which made him feel both important and a little self-conscious. Still, Kun could sense, beneath the words, such a tone of longing that he found himself feeling angry with Liang for not visiting more, and defensive of Zhao Yubi, who was trying so hard to sound cheerful.

When they finished, Zhao Yubi surprised him by saying that she was tired and needed to rest. Clio sent him home early, with the letter to mail on the way.

Kun was unusually quiet at dinner. His father, who had been congratulating himself on the success of his plan, was puzzled. Until today, Kun had returned from the Home happy and energized. Still, he hoped Kun would confide in him without his having to pry. Kun retired silently to his room.

Giving in to curiosity and concern, Baba tapped on Kun's door and entered the room. Kun sat at his desk, absentmindedly doodling in the margins of a school assignment.

"Is everything OK, son? You've been very quiet."

Kun jumped, startled.

"Oh, it's nothing, Baba."

"I don't think it's nothing. Until today, you've come back from Yixian excited and full of stories. Today, nothing. What's on your mind?"

"I'm not sure, really. Instead of telling stories today, Zhao Yubi had me write a letter to her son for her. She's usually so lively and fun, even when she's grouchy. But today, writing the letter, even though she tried to be happy, she seemed sad. Afterwards, she was tired and went to bed. I think she really misses her son. Why doesn't he visit her more?"

Baba sat on Kun's bed. "I don't know. Maybe he really can't."

The two sat for a while. Finally Kun spoke up, anger in his voice.

"I think he should visit her more. If she were my mother or grandmother, I wouldn't leave her alone to miss me like that. I'd want to visit her and make sure she was OK."

Kun's father smiled slightly at the irony of the situation. Tempting as it was to point out the connection between what Kun was experiencing and the incident that got him in trouble in the first place, he chose to let the words hang in the air, hoping Kun would figure it out for himself. He said goodnight and left the room.

On the way to the Home on Thursday, Kun sped along eagerly. He parked his bike, pulled a tape recorder out of his bag, and trotted in the door and down the hall, waving at Clio on the way.

"Wait a second!" Clio called. "You look cheerful. What's up? I was concerned that you might be worried about Zhao Yubi after your last visit. You seemed upset."

"Maybe a little. But I have an idea that will cheer her up. Is she ready for me?"

"Ready and waiting. Mind if I sit in with you today?"

"I guess that's OK," Kun responded. He didn't feel he could say no, but he was a little disappointed. He hadn't thought about sharing his time with ZhaoYubi and he wasn't sure he liked the idea.

"Great! I'm curious about this idea of yours. Lead the way."

Zhao Yubi was waiting, as Clio said. Kun noticed that she had on her bright red lipstick again, and her cheeks were pink. She waved him in with impatience. At the same moment, host and visitor exploded with excited greetings:

"I have an idea!" shouted Kun.

"I have a surprise for you!" chirped Zhao Yubi.

All three laughed. "You first, boy," Zhao Yubi commanded. "What's your idea?"

"Well, I like your stories so much, and drawing pictures to

go with them, that I brought a tape recorder. That way I can work more on the pictures after I leave and even use your words with them to tell the story, like in a comic strip. Maybe you could even record more stories between our visits, if you want, for me to listen to and work on at home. What do you think?"

Zhao Yubi flushed with pleasure. "I think that's a fine idea! My words and your pictures make a wonderful way to share these stories. And I know just where to start."

"But what's your surprise?"

"My surprise will be the first story we work on together, to share with the world! But let me back up a little. My son got our letter and called last night. He's going to try to visit me next month! I'm grateful to you for helping me. I decided to thank you by setting you straight about General Yue Fei. As I recall, you called him a 'foolish old mama's boy?' So I did a little brushing up on him, and today I want to tell you part of his story."

Kun, embarrassed by the reminder of his transgression, busied himself setting up the recorder and gathering paper and pens before announcing, "All ready. Set me straight!"

Zhao Yubi launched into the story, as animated as the first time Kun met her. He had to sketch hastily to keep up with her—these drawings would need a lot of finishing! But her spirited telling brought the story to life from the first word. When she came to the part about young Yue Fei's dilemma about whether he should leave to fight with the army defending his country from invaders or stay behind to take care of his elderly mother, she spoke with piercing eyes and poignant drama. She made Kun feel the anguish of the General's conflict of duties and appreciate the honorable character revealed by that pain. What should Yue Fei do? Which duty was more important?

Kun even forgot to draw, so caught up was he in the drama Zhao Yubi described. She paused theatrically; then went on.

"...And how did General Yue Fei resolve his conflict? His mother, in a spectacular act of courage and heroism, did what no mother ever wants to do. She tattooed four words on her son's back: 'jing zhong bao guo,' meaning 'Serve the country loyally,' making it clear that her wish was for him to fulfill his destiny as a soldier and a patriot! She sent her son to war to relieve him of the burden of his dilemma."

Clio jumped up excitedly. "That makes me think of Thetis, Achilles' mother, who tried every magic she could to keep her son from dying a soldier's death!" [3]

Zhao Yubi and Kun scowled at Clio for interrupting. Clio apologized, adding one last thought in homage to the General's mother: "Except Thetis never did understand Achilles' duty as a soldier. So I guess this general's mother was more heroic...." Her words trailed off, and Zhao Yubi finished her story.

"General Yue Fei went on to a glorious military career as a general undefeated in battle. But just as importantly, he has remained, to this day, a symbol of faithfulness, loyalty, and compassion, for his fair treatment of enemies and his kind, generous concern for the men in his command and their families."

Zhao Yubi stopped, and slumped a little in her chair from the physical and emotional effort expended in telling the story. She looked directly at Kun.

"Would you agree, boy, that there is no 'foolish mama's boy' in this story? And that, in fact, there are two heroes here, not just one?"

"Yes, Zhao Nai-Nai," Kun whispered meekly. "Thank you for setting me straight."

The weeks passed quickly. Kun biked to the Home twice, sometimes three times, a week. Zhao Yubi told stories, while he sketched rapidly. He left the recorder with her, and now and then, after a meeting of the storytelling group, she'd present him with extra stories on tape. She wove her spell as she recounted thrilling tales of the young female heroine Hua Mulan [4], Protector General Ban Chao [5], and more. Kun rushed through his homework each night, in order to concentrate on adapting Zhao Yubi's spoken words into comic strips. She was critical at first, doubting that so few words could really tell the stories. But Kun showed her samples of comic books and graphic novels. Gradually, shaping the comic strips with him, she was convinced, especially when Kun told her that he had shown their work to Teacher Yang, the one he'd gotten in trouble with. His teacher was thrilled, and said she'd look into getting one of their stories published in the school newspaper.

In the back of Kun's mind, he was vaguely aware that Zhao Yubi was weakening. As time passed, he often found her slack and diminished, until storytelling brought her to sparkling, energetic life. But because most of the time they spent together showed her at her best, he refused to acknowledge the worry tapping at the edges of his awareness.

Clio joined them most days, now. She watched and encouraged the partnership with both delight and apprehension. *No worries about my mission,* she thought. *Kun has already learned everything he needs to fire his passion and use his art to share his people's history. But I can't leave now! Clearly, this can't go on much longer. What will happen to Kun when Zhao Yubi can no longer give him the words?*

Kun didn't even notice when his month of "punishment" was up. He biked to the Home after school as usual, this time armed with the best surprise of all—the news that his school newspaper would print their graphic version of the story of General Yue Fei in installments over the next few weeks! And who knows? Maybe more after that. He'd have skipped checking in with Clio entirely, but she was waiting for him at the entrance. Her expression made him instantly wary.

"Kun, I'm afraid I have bad news. Zhao Yubi is gone."

Confused, Kun stammered, "Gone? What do you mean, gone? Did her son come and take her to Chengdu to live?"

"No, Kun. I mean she died. She was ninety-one, and she'd gotten so frail and weak. It happened just this afternoon. I didn't know how to reach you, but I knew you'd be coming to see her. I'm sorry, Kun."

Kun could hardly take it in. *Gone? Dead?*

"That can't be! She was just telling me stories on Thursday. She was fine!"

"She wasn't really fine, Kun. But she always perked up when you came. The only time she was lively like that is when you visited and she told stories. You must have noticed, even so, that she was getting weaker."

Clio was almost pleading with him now, willing him to take it in, and not be as hurt as she knew he would be.

"I didn't even get to say goodbye to her! Why didn't she wait to say goodbye?"

Kun was crying now. Clio, not known for sensitivity to those around her, felt her heart go out to him. She put an arm across his shoulder. He pulled away.

In a flash of insight, Clio suggested, "I think she didn't want you to see her weak and helpless. She wanted you to remember her full of energy and heroic stories."

Torn between grief and anger, he shouted, "Her son never even visited! He let her die without even seeing him again!"

"Try not to be too angry, Kun. He really was planning to visit next month. But the important thing is that she wasn't lonely in her last weeks. And that's because of you."

"Me? But she fussed, and scolded me! She got impatient with me all the time!"

"And she felt useful having someone to fuss over and scold. It was just her way. She loved the time you had together, passing her stories on to you."

Kun thought about Clio's words and knew, underneath all the pain and dismay and anger, that they were true.

"Why don't you go to her room? She's not there, but maybe it would give you a chance to sort of say goodbye. I think she left something there for you."

Kun nodded and headed down the hall with shuffling steps and lowered eyes.

About half an hour later, Clio led Kun's father into Zhao Yubi's room.

"I hope you don't mind, Kun. I called your father to come and get you."

Kun, perched on his usual bench across from the empty wheelchair, shrugged. He held a thick, worn, old book in his lap, rubbing the rough edges of the bumpy leather binding absently with his thumb. There was an envelope sticking out that had his name on it.

His father spoke first.

"I'm so sorry, son. I know Zhao Yubi meant a lot to you. What do you have there?"

Kun handed him the book. On the envelope, almost unreadable in Zhao Yubi's shaky writing, were these words: "For Kun. I leave it to you to keep these stories of old fools and mama's boys alive."

Baba showed the envelope to Clio and the two shared a small smile over the inscription.

"Let's go home, son. It's nearly dinnertime. Didn't you tell me your fist comic strip about Yue Fei is due tomorrow?"

Kun looked up, pain and confusion in his eyes. "Comic strip? I can't do the comic strips without Zhao Nai-Nai! It's all about her words. There's no story without her words."

"But, Kun, you have to!" Clio protested. "Look at her message. She wanted you to keep sharing the stories, in your own way—through your pictures. You already have some stories taped in her words, and now you have this whole book. You change the words, anyway, to work with the drawings."

"But it's Zhao Nai-Nai that made the stories seem real and exciting."

"She certainly did that." Baba spoke softly, as he laid a hand on Kun's shoulder. "And now I think it's your job to make them real and exciting to other young people. She left you both a legacy and a dying wish. Remember, you came here to learn proper respect for your culture and your heritage. I believe it's your duty to honor Zhao Yubi by fulfilling her wish."

Kun looked up at Baba and Clio. Both smiled and nodded at him. He stood up, holding the book to his chest.

"Let's go, then," he said.

They were almost home when Kun, who had not spoken, surprised his father with a request.

"Baba, I meant it when I said we're fine as we are and I don't need a mother. But do you think we could go visit my Nai-Nai more often?"

Baba nodded. "I think we can do that."

Footnotes
1. During the Song Dynasty, Yue Fei was a great General in defense of his country. He was never defeated in battle. He was also celebrated as a symbol of loyalty and faithfulness, as Zhao Yubi explains in her story.
2. Nai-Nai is Chinese (Mandarin) for grandmother. It is also used, with a family name, to refer to any respected elderly woman.
3. Thetis, an immortal sea nymph and mother of Achilles, worried because her son was half mortal. Upon hearing that he was fated to die in battle, she took extreme measures to protect him. She dipped him in the river Styx to try to make him immortal, dressed him as a girl when he was a child and hid him away on an island, and had a magic sword and shield made for him. While Achilles loved and respected his mother all his life, he couldn't avoid his destiny. He died a hero in the Trojan War, despite all her efforts.
4. In ancient China, Hua Mulan disguised herself as a man and took her sick, elderly father's place, fighting invaders in the Emperor's army. She fought with distinction and was made a general, all without revealing her identity. When the war was over, Mulan dropped her disguise and refused riches to return home and live simply.
5. Protector General Ban Chao was a venerated diplomat and soldier during the Han Dynasty, who brought Central Asia back under Chinese rule and protected traffic on the Silk Road trade route.

CHAPTER 9

TERPSICHORE'S MISSION: FIFTY DANCING ELEPHANTS

For you, Terpsichore, Muse of dance and creative movement, I've found a special challenge. A young girl in Russia, despite a great ballet heritage and impressive talent, resents the pressure to excel. Between family problems and a competing passion for animals, she's in danger of turning her back on her artistic calling. You must help her find a way to be true to her distinctive gifts.

St. Petersburg, Russia

"Now, children, fourth position. We'll work on our pirouettes [1] for the remainder of today's class. Eyes front; chins up."

Madam Bogdanova circled the studio with eagle eyes, correcting a stance here, a technique there.

"Veronika, where **is** your mind today? You're only first year, I realize, but soon you'll be ready to go on pointe and these movements should feel as natural to you as breathing!

138

You should be far ahead of the other ten-year-olds. Your Papa would be so distressed. He was never distracted in class!"

Nika blinked back tears. She loved to dance—really, she did! And sometimes it did feel as natural as breathing. But how could she concentrate, knowing that her favorite dog at the animal shelter might die at any moment—might even be dead already? She'd thought of little else all day.

After class, Veronika hurriedly changed clothes, stuffed her practice leotard and shoes into her bag, and sprinted for the door. She just **had** to know if Dozor made it through the night. She ran for the metro station, hoping with all her might that the new medicine would work and the dog would recover.

She entered the Red Village Shelter, as she did every Tuesday afternoon, and raced to the infirmary in the back. As she pushed through the door, her view of the examining table was blocked by Dr. Ivanov's bulky frame. But he heard her enter and stepped back with a smile, revealing a weak, but clear-eyed, large red mutt who yipped a greeting.

"Dozor, you're OK! Is he really going to be OK, Doc? I can't believe it!" As she hugged the homely dog, with tears in her eyes, Doctor Ivanov nodded.

"Yes, I believe he will. I'm relieved. I don't know if I could stand another scene like the one you made when that kitten died last month. Really, Nika, I worry about you. You're too soft-hearted for this job! We can't save them all, you know, and I can't have you falling apart every time we lose an animal. Are you sure you wouldn't be happier volunteering at the food pantry?"

"No! I need to be here. I want to be a veterinarian like you someday, so I need to learn all I can. I'll be tougher, I promise."

Doctor Ivanov's brow furrowed. "Does your mother know of this new ambition? I suspect she has other plans for you."

"Of course she does. Everyone has 'other plans' for me— the only child of the great Maxim Popov! But I'll never be as good a dancer as Papa, and it's animals I care about most."

"Ah, well, it's good of your mother to let you come here. You do have a way with the animals. Every one of them perks up when you arrive. Why don't you take over brushing Dozor while I check on our other patients?"

Nika let herself into the flat. Mama was dusting a large framed photograph of Nika's father, gracefully executing a perfect arabesque on stage. Nika clenched her fists. *Here she goes again,* Nika thought, *acting like he was the greatest thing ever!* When her parents divorced four years before, her mother had angrily removed all photos—all traces, really—of her father's presence from the apartment. The divorce had been almost a relief, Nika remembered. Papa hadn't ever been around much, and when he was, he and Mama argued constantly. But when he died suddenly, almost eighteen months ago, Mama grieved like a broken-hearted widow. She hung this portrait in prominent view and talked to anyone who would listen about her beloved Maxim. To hear her talk, you'd never know that the couple had ever been at odds, let alone divorced. It disgusted Nika.

Mama heard Nika enter, sighed dramatically, and turned to greet her.

"How was dance today, darling? Is your pirouette improving?"

"Dozor is much better, Mama, thank you for asking!" Nika stomped down the hall to her room. *That's just like her, to think only about herself, and her plans for me to dance like Papa and make her look good! She doesn't even care, doesn't even remember about Dozor, or what's important to me!*

Mama knocked at the door and opened it. She seemed chastened, smaller than her usual imposing self.

"Dozor must be that dog you told me about at the Shelter," she offered. "I'm glad he's better, Nika. But I worry that you're spending too much time there and it's taking away from your focus on ballet. You have such talent! You're so privileged to study at Vaganova Academy, and you know your Papa would have wanted…"

"I don't **care** what Papa would have wanted!" Nika's tall, slender body tightened as she turned on her mother with anger. "And you didn't care, either, until he died and everyone made such a fuss over him. It's like you've forgotten what he was really like! You just like all the attention you get from having been his wife, and you want me to be just like him so the attention keeps coming! What about what I want? What about what matters to me?"

"This is how you talk to me? This is how you treat me, when all I want is for you to develop your talent and have every opportunity?" She turned and stormed out of the room.

Nika's anger evaporated as quickly as it had formed. She slumped into a chair. *Why does everyone think I should be like my father? So what if he was a great dancer, and* **so** *charming. I'm not him! I hardly even knew him. Even if I could be as good a dancer, I don't want to be like him, and I don't know why Mama wants me to be.*

Dinner was silent, the flavor of the piroshka and borscht [2] soured by hurt feelings and resentment.

When Nika arrived at the Shelter the next week, Dr. Ivanov introduced her to a young woman named Chorie. Like Nika, she was tall, with long legs and a long neck; about twenty, Nika guessed. Black-haired and pretty, with pale skin and bright lavender eyes.

"Chorie will be volunteering here for a while, as part of her program at Smolny College. She's newly arrived from Greece. I told her she should watch you and take her cues from our number one volunteer, Veronika Popova!"

"Nice to meet you. Doc, can I go see Dozor? How is he?"

"He's much better, and I'm sure he's waiting for you. Go on, and check back with me when you've finished your usual chores."

Later, as Nika was making a last round before heading home, she stopped to visit Ptichka, the Shelter's cockatiel mascot. Ptichka swayed rhythmically on his perch, as if dancing to the music playing softly in the background. Nika began to sway and dip around the empty waiting room, in improvised mimicry of the bird's movement. She added a demi-plie and a releve, giggling. As she pirouetted, she noticed Chorie watching her from the doorway. She blushed, and paused self-consciously.

"No, don't stop!" said Chorie. "It's lovely. I'll join you!" She began her own graceful interpretation of the bird's motions. As the music changed to a livelier tune, Ptichka, Nika, and Chorie all responded. Soon the three were happily sharing a spontaneous fusion of traditional and popular dance.

When they finally collapsed, breathless, Nika asked, "You're a dancer?"

"And not the only one in the room," Chorie laughed, nodding toward both the girl and the bird. "You're obviously talented and trained, yourself."

"I've studied ballet ever since I was three. My father was a famous dancer, so it's kind of expected."

"More than expected, I think. You dance with such grace and joy!"

"Well," Nika admitted, "that's the most fun I've had dancing in a long time. I'm afraid my ballet teacher would not be pleased, though. The choreography didn't exactly follow classical tradition!"

"Surely, she wants you to enjoy yourself when you dance, right?"

"I'm not sure that enjoying myself is her concern. She's very strict."

"She probably just wants you to be the best dancer you can be. And I'm guessing that would be very, very good."

"How can you tell? We're practically strangers and that wasn't exactly a demonstration of ballet basics!"

"Really, Veronika, how can you say we're practically strangers, after sharing a dance like that? I'd say that qualifies us as good friends! As for how I can tell about your talent, I've also danced ever since I could walk, and that makes me a great deal more experienced than you! I've taught as well as studied dance, and it's obvious that you're no ordinary prima ballerina wannabe. So why aren't you having more fun?"

As Nika and Chorie walked together from the Shelter, across the Moika Bridge and along the canal to the metro station, Nika found herself telling Chorie about her life—her gifted, but distant, dead father; her self-centered mother; her love for animals; and her doubts about where dance fit in her life. It felt good to have a grown-up listen with real interest! Chorie waited with her for the bus, and by the time it arrived

Nika felt a little embarrassed about revealing so much of herself.

"Will you be at the Shelter next week? Then you can tell me more about you. I talked too much today."

"I'll be there. And don't worry. I remember being your age and I can relate to family pressures. I loved hearing about you. Maybe we can get Ptichka to dance with us again next week."

"I'd like that! See you then." Nika boarded the bus, feeling better than she had in a long time.

The happiness didn't last. During the next week, Nika felt more pressure than ever, both at home and at Vaganova Academy. Auditions for roles in the first-year students' performance were approaching. Mama and Madam Bogdanova agreed that Maxim Popov's daughter should certainly dance the leading girl's role, and pushed her constantly to practice. When Mama suggested, over breakfast one morning, that Nika take a break from the Shelter to concentrate on rehearsal until after auditions, Nika snapped.

"**No**! It's never enough! I'll never be good enough, even if I practice day and night. Maybe I don't even want the leading role! Did you ever think of that? I'm not going to give up the Shelter! You can't make me!" She spun on her heel, and stomped off to school, leaving her mother standing, stunned, at the door of the flat.

Tuesday came around again. Nika was angry and tired. All she wanted was to get to the Shelter to see Doc, Dozer, and Ptichka. And Chorie. She hurried along, the blustery wind chilling her. Would Chorie be there? Would she want to spend time with Nika again? Chorie was young, but she was a grown-up. In Nika's experience, grown-ups were usually demanding and unreliable. Was it too much to hope that this one might really care about her? She sighed with relief when she entered the Shelter. The warm air wrapped around her. Welcoming gestures from staff and eager affection from the animals cheered her, as she greeted them one by one. She didn't see Chorie before Doc sent her out to clean up the yard, but as she reentered the building she heard someone calling her name.

"Hi! Doc has lots for me to do today and I got slowed down by a strange visit with one of my sisters," Chorie said, "so I don't think I'll have time for a dance with you and Ptichka. But would you like to go for a lemonade when we're done? I have something to show you."

"Yes! But I have to be sure to catch my ride. Mama will be upset if I'm late," she answered, rolling her eyes. She was pleased with Chorie's interest, and definitely curious.

"What is it?"

"Not now. I'll show you later."

As they sat sipping their sweet drinks, Nika fidgeted. Chorie had a large bag resting against her leg, but she chatted randomly about the animals at the Shelter. The twinkle in her eye made Nika suspect that Chorie was teasing her, purposely feeding her curiosity. But after talking so much the week before, Nika didn't dare push. Instead, she asked Chorie polite questions about herself.

"Yes, I come from a big family. And, yes, my sisters did study dance with me, though I'm told that I'm the best dancer among them. My sisters have many talents. But enough about me!" She grinned and lifted the bag. "I can see you're bursting to know what I brought for you. Here it is. Do you read English well?"

"Pretty well," Nika answered, as Chorie pulled out a picture book and handed it to her. The front cover showed the title, *Ballet of the Elephants* [3], and a picture of four ballerinas dancing in front of an elephant in a sort of tutu. Nika laughed delightedly. "What is this? A dancing elephant? How funny! Who thought up such a silly thing?"

"Silly, yes," replied Chorie, "but also true! There were actually fifty dancing elephants! And two of the three people who thought it up were famous artists from right here in St. Petersburg. You've heard of George Balanchine, right? He studied at your Academy."

Nika's eyes widened. "Of course! They say he was the best choreographer in the world."

"And how about the composer, Igor Stravinsky? You might have danced to his music."

144

"Yes, though Madam Bogdanova doesn't like him much. He's not nearly traditional enough for her. But what do they have to do with dancing elephants?"

Chorie explained, as they paged through the book together. "In the 1940s an American named John Ringling North ran a circus. He got a wild idea about creating an act with dancing elephants. Balanchine and Stravinsky had both moved to America and become friends. North approached Balanchine about helping him, and Balanchine asked Stravinsky to write the music. They did it! It was part polka, part waltz, and part ballet featuring fifty elephants and fifty ballerinas, and it was performed over four hundred times in America."

Now Nika's eyes were huge. "No! You're teasing me, right?"

"I'm serious. Read for yourself. It's my book; you can borrow it if you like."

"Thanks! That's about the best thing I ever heard of! Maybe we should hire a composer and make a dance for Ptichka and the animals at the Shelter," she giggled. "Wouldn't that be a sight? It would give Mama and Madam Bogdanova fits!"

Chorie laughed with her.

"It probably would, but what fun it would be! We know we have a willing dancer in Ptichka. Who knows what hidden talents Dozor and the others might have, just waiting to be discovered?"

They parted chuckling. All the way home, Nika's head was filled with images of elephants, dogs, cats, and birds waltzing across a stage to a lilting tune.

Though she knew it was ridiculous, Nika couldn't shake the idea of choreographing a dance for the Shelter animals. In her room that night, when she should have been resting in anticipation of next week's auditions, her imagination raced. One by one, the animals popped into her mind and she began to analyze, and then mimic with her body, how each moved. The vague music in her mind changed with each animal— somber and elegant for the elderly wolfhound Dora, syncopated and sprightly for the newly-arrived rabbit, and so on. She couldn't sleep for the exhilaration. Suddenly, she remembered something. What was that music she'd heard a fourth year student dancing to? Something about animals... something about swans... or a circus or—that's it! A carnival! *Carnival of the Animals* [4], by some French composer. Saint-something. She'd look for it tomorrow. In the back of her mind, a plan was taking shape.

Meanwhile, Chorie sat sipping tea in the tiny flat she'd rented, just down Rossi Street from the Academy. She pondered her next move. *Nika's talented, for sure,* she thought, *and so eager for someone to pay real attention to her. I think I sort of understand her. We both have strong-willed mothers with high expectations and not a lot of interest in what we think or want. We get along great and she seems open to anything I say. So... what should I say? How can I encourage her to use her talents in ways that interest her, without upsetting her training and causing more problems at home? If I don't think of something soon, I'm going to have to call for help.*

Later that week, Madam Bogdanova stopped to watch closely, as Nika rehearsed the dance the teacher had chosen for her audition. For the first time in weeks, she liked what she saw.

"Ah, Nika, that's much better! Almost worthy of the daughter of Maxim Popov! See what happens when you focus? When you give it your best, I don't believe another pupil in the first or second year can touch you. Keep at it and your audition will be excellent."

"Thank you, Madam Bogdanova. I do want to be excellent." Nika smiled a private smile, savoring her own secret plans. How funny, that all her work to prepare her audition surprise seemed to be making her better in class, as well!

Chorie and Nika sat in the café sipping hot chocolate, the next Tuesday. Nika had just finished telling Chorie about remembering the "Swan" piece from *Carnival of the Animals,* and borrowing a DVD of it from the Academy library. Her voice rose with excitement as she described it.

"Do you know it? The "Swan" piece is beautiful, but some of the other parts remind me so much of dancing with Ptichka that day—they're such fun, and the music fits each animal perfectly!"

"Of course! I do know it, and I can't believe I didn't think to share it with you myself! It's perfect for you, with your two loves. I'm glad you found it. Which part do you like best?"

"I love it all, but I think I like the birds one, 'Aviary,' best."

Nika turned her eyes away and smiled mysteriously. The conversation faltered.

Chorie filled the unusual silence with a change of subject. "Isn't your big audition coming up soon?"

"Yes, it's a week from Saturday. Will you come and watch? It's open and I think it's going to be really good!"

Again, Nika smiled slightly, and looked away.

Chorie tilted her head, sensing there was more to the story. "I'd love to. I'm glad you're excited about it."

"I am. I think you'll be surprised."

"Seeing you dance well won't surprise me at all."

"Just come, OK? I should go catch the bus."

"I'll be there." As Chorie made her way home, she wondered about Nika's strange behavior, but quickly put it out of her mind. *I'm just glad she's looking forward to the audition. Maybe I've helped her feel better about dancing already.*

Chorie sat in the auditorium on audition day, watching Nika's classmates deliver skilled, but unremarkable, performances and feeling satisfied that she'd steered Nika well. *Nika's better than any of these and she seems happy about dancing again. Maybe she just needed someone to listen to her and encourage both of her interests, to show her that she didn't have to choose between them. Maybe, after today, I should head home and see how the others have done with their missions. Could it be that easy? Maybe I'm just good at this sort of thing! I should ask Mother for another mission.*

Madam Bogdanova introduced Veronika Popov and

returned to her chair, far to the right of the stage. She smiled encouragingly and nodded at Nika, who waited in the opposite wing. Chorie sat up straight, aiming a cell phone camera to record the performance. After all, she'd be going home soon, and she'd become fond of spunky, determined Nika. This way, she could pull up the video anytime she found herself missing the girl. After a short delay, Nika entered the stage with both arms full. Chorie watched as three things happened in quick succession. Nika carried Ptichka (of all things!) to the piano and set him on the back of the music stand. She lifted a feathery headdress she carried in the other arm and placed it on her head. And then the music began. It was "Aviary," from *Carnival of the Animals!* Nika began to dance to the fluttery music. She bobbed and swayed, combining classic ballet steps with elements of jazz, and even hip-hop, in an enchanting, but startlingly non-traditional expression of the spirit of a whole range of birds much less stately and graceful than the Swan. Ptichka danced with her from his perch on the piano. This **was** a surprise, but not, it seemed, a welcome one to everyone.

Chorie continued to record, as her delight gave way to concern. Madam Bogdanova jumped up from her chair, a vein in her neck bulging and fury on her face. She sat back down, but every muscle in her body screamed shock and anger. At the same time, a woman at the end of the front row, whom Chorie assumed must be Nika's mother, also rose to her feet, her expression a combination of bewilderment and alarm. She remained standing in the aisle, mouth agape and hands palm out in dismay.

Oh, Nika! What have you done? Chorie thought. Clearly, neither Madam Bogdanova nor Mrs. Popova knew about this. *It's a surprise, alright, and a dangerous one!* Realizing that she had stopped recording as the shock registered, she quickly raised her phone to continue. As surely as she knew this situation was bad, she realized that the dance was good. Very good. She was helpless to do anything but admire Nika's talent and daring, and keep recording. She glanced around the audience. A few parents and faculty members fidgeted in their seats and whispered to each other, but most were completely enthralled, moving their heads along with Nika, Ptichka, and the music. *She's brilliant,* Chorie realized. *She's a little bird-woman, but the opposite of a Harpy* [5]—*sweet and beautiful!*

The music ended and Nika took a bow. Madam Bogdanova had no choice but to try to appear calm and introduce the next dancer with as much dignity as she could muster; Mrs. Popova stalked out of the auditorium.

Full marks for sheer nerve, Nika, but I don't envy you the consequences. How angry will they be? Chorie wondered. *What will they do to you?*

As soon as the last dancer finished, Chorie hurried out of the auditorium in the direction Mrs. Popova had gone. Heading down a long hallway, she heard muffled shouts coming from a room ahead. She peeked through the window. Mrs. Popova was shrieking at Nika, looking like she might explode at any moment. Nika was trying to look properly repentant, but her eyes were clear and her posture confident. Nika glanced up, saw Chorie watching them, and gave her a little wave. Then she shooed Chorie away.

Chorie couldn't stand not knowing what was happening to Nika. She desperately wanted to talk to her, but she could hardly show up at Nika's flat uninvited. She waited nervously for Tuesday, putting in extra hours at the Shelter to keep busy. On Monday, Nika came there looking for her.

Chorie hugged Nika, then held her shoulders and faced her.

"How are you? What's happened to you? Did you get in terrible trouble? That dance was brilliant, but you weren't kidding when you said I'd be surprised. And I wasn't the only one! What were you thinking? How could you take such a risk?"

Nika's lip quivered and tears filled her eyes.

"They're threatening to kick me out of the Academy! Madam Bogdanova thought I was making fun of her and the school! She and Mama are so mad. I really wasn't trying to make them look bad, but I'm not sorry! I had to change the dance. Wait... Did you say it was brilliant?"

Her teary eyes widened as the message sank in.

"Yes. It was brilliant, but if I'd known, I'd never have let you take such a big chance."

"**Let** me? It wasn't up to you! You didn't tell me to do it, but I had to. How else could I get them to pay attention to what I want? How could I convince them that I'm a dancer, but I'm not like Papa? I **am** a dancer, Chorie, and I want to study and be the best I can be. But I had to do it. I'm not sorry. And wasn't Ptichka wonderful?"

Chorie shook her head and laughed softly.

"He was. And you were. I can't believe you took such a risk or that you're still determined in spite of everything. You are so strong!"

"Strong, maybe. But what am I going to do? Even if they don't kick me out, I can't go back there and study the way my father did, the way they want me to. But I need to study and I need to keep doing what I did on Saturday."

"How are things at home?"

"Worse than I thought they'd be. I didn't know she'd be quite so mad. I knew I wasn't doing what they wanted, but I thought it would make them see what I want, what I can do. Mama goes back and forth between shouting about how I betrayed 'Dear Papa,' and falling into swoons worthy of the theatre. She's enjoying the drama, so I'm just trying to stay out of her way."

"What if I told them it was my fault, that I encouraged you?"

"But that's not true! All you did was listen to me and show me that dance could be something different. Besides, they wouldn't care. They can't see the good in anything that's not traditional."

"We'll figure something out. Give me a little time to think. Will you be here next week?"

"Nothing could stop me!"

"I believe you! Here's my phone number. Call me if anything drastic happens."

Chorie paced her small room, racking her brain for an idea—any idea—of how to fix this mess. Could there be a solution that made everyone happy, especially Nika? Hard as she tried, nothing came to her. It was time to call for help. *Who should I call? Not Calliope or Clio. They'd just yell at me for "creating a monster." Maybe Erato? She's not so superior, but she's vain enough to relate to Madam Bogdanova and Mrs. Popova. Maybe she can help me find a way to appease them.*

Chorie signaled for her sister, tapping her finger tips. Almost immediately, Erato appeared beside her, smoothing her dark brown hair and looking around.

"Don't you have a mirror around here somewhere? That whirlwind trip messed up my braid, I'm sure!"

"Oh, Era, forget your hair! I really need your help. I thought things were going so well, and then my girl pulled a stunt that could end her dance career before it even begins! I need you to help me sort this out."

"Fine. Don't panic. How bad could it be? We'll figure it out and then I can get back to my own mission. I'm rather enjoying it, I must say! So tell me what's happening."

Chorie did just that. As she brought Era up to the present, Era interrupted her.

"She really did that? The girl has guts, I'll give her that! Maybe more guts than brains, but still…"

Chorie puffed up with pride for her talented, passionate, daring young friend.

"Yes, but that's almost the best thing about her! Whatever I do, I can't try to make her give in. If there were only some way to get Madam Bogdanova and the others at the Academy to realize how good she is and to let her be herself!"

"That doesn't sound likely. But why does she have to stay at the Academy? This is Russia! There must be other good dance studios around."

"Not like this one! It's the premiere place in the world to study traditional, classic ballet. Nika needs the best."

"Maybe the best, but best at what? I'm not seeing Nika's destiny in traditional, classic ballet. Are you? Who's the best at contemporary dance? Who's the best at giving promising young dancers room to do their own thing? I think Nika needs a better 'best' for her."

"Maybe you're onto something."

Chorie pulled out her phone and started surfing the Internet for dance academies in St. Petersburg. Heads together, the sisters checked out link after link, studio after studio. It didn't take long to discover a promising fit.

"Look, Era—Kannon Dance. I've heard of it. It has a wonderful reputation for improvisation and innovative choreography. Its annual Open Look Festival features experimental pieces and nontraditional dancers from all over the world."

As the two read on, Chorie's excitement grew.

"This looks tailor-made for Nika. They'd appreciate her and she'd be in her element. It's perfect!"

"Well, there you go, then. I guess I'll be off. I have a handsome young poet swooning over me. I need to get back to Italy."

"Wait! Not so fast! It's one thing to decide that Kannon is the place for Nika, but quite another thing to get her there! Even if we could get them to invite her to study there, how would we ever convince her mother? Mrs. Popova wants the glory of continuing Nika's father's legacy. She won't be eager to break with tradition. And even if she were, would Madam Bogdanova really let the daughter of the great Maxim Popov go?"

"Easy, Sis! Slow down. One problem at a time. Let's start with Kannon. You said you videotaped Nika's audition, right? Give me your phone. I need to check out Kannon's faculty. I have an idea. It's a little risky, but I don't think it technically breaks Mother's rules. And after the risk Nika took, I think pushing the boundaries a little might be in order."

It was late when Chorie and Erato put the finishing touches on their plan and gave each other a hug for luck.

"Do we really dare, Era? If we make Mother mad we could ruin things for everyone."

"Think about it. Mother's tough, but fair. And what she said was 'you will work with your young mortals only through ordinary interaction....' That's **your** young mortals. That means the kids she chose for us, right? She didn't say anything about **other** mortals. And the only sure way to win over the girl's mother is to give her a huge dose of flattery. We'll conjure up something worthy of Aphrodite [6]."

"But a love potion is so... well..."

Before Chorie could finish the sentence, Erato snapped her fingers and disappeared. Chorie paced her small apartment, just as she had earlier in the evening, but this time with nervous anticipation rather than dismay. Kannon Dance wouldn't be open until morning, but she wasn't at all sleepy. She couldn't wait to set the plan in motion!

The next afternoon Mr. Borodin, Director of Kannon Dance, returned from a meeting to find a large envelope on his desk. In it were three things—a DVD, a piece of the expensive chocolate he favored, and a note. The note read:

"I believe you will be intensely interested in this performance by a most promising young dancer, who happens to be the daughter of the great, late Maxim Popov. She has been studying at Vaganova Academy, but I have it on good authority that she may be looking to transfer to an institution more in keeping with her particular talent. You'll want to act quickly, before some less worthy institution steals her from you. I'm offering you this information anonymously, as it would be unwise for one of my stature in the world of dance to be seen playing favorites with the great academies. But be advised—this rare opportunity is to be taken seriously! P.S. The sweet is to demonstrate that I am someone who knows you and the elite of Russia's dance community very well."

There was no signature. Intrigued, Mr. Borodin slid the DVD into his computer drive.

Twenty minutes later, the Director of Kannon Dance left the building. Popping the chocolate in his mouth, he hailed a taxi.

Mrs. Popova heard a knock and opened the door to find a handsome, middle-aged man standing on the stoop, holding a large bouquet of flowers. She recognized him, of course. Everyone in St. Petersburg involved with dance knew about him. Whatever could he be doing at her door?

Borodin's eyes widened when he saw Mrs. Popova.

"Good day, Madam. I am Mark Borodin, Director of

Kannon Dance. These are for you," he announced, bowing elegantly as he handed her the flowers. "I hope I'm not intruding, but I have urgent business to discuss with you."

His voice trailed off, and he gazed intently into the woman's eyes.

"Yes?" she replied. "Please come in, sir. May I offer you tea?"

"Thank you. I'd be delighted."

He followed her into the sitting room and waited while she busied herself in the kitchen. He couldn't seem to think clearly. He'd seen Popov's widow now and then over the years, of course, but somehow he hadn't remembered her being so beautiful or charming.

Mrs. Popova returned and poured the tea.

"What brings you here, Mr. Borodin?"

"What's that?" Mr. Borodin mumbled, staring at her.

"What business brings you here?"

"Oh, yes. Forgive me. I do have important business to discuss with you. But first, let me tell you what an honor and privilege it is to meet the lovely wife of the esteemed Maxim Popov! I knew he was a talented man, but I didn't realize what a lucky man he was, as well. You are really quite enchanting. But people must tell you that all the time."

Mrs. Popova blushed and dropped her eyes coyly. She found Mr. Borodin decidedly better-looking than his pictures in the press.

"How kind of you! But truly, the honor is mine, as a simple patron of the arts."

"Nonsense! You no doubt inspired Maxim, and now it seems you have produced another inspiring gift to the art world."

"What do you mean?"

"I'm referring to your daughter, Veronika. An anonymous friend sent me a recording of your daughter's recent performance of the Saint-Saens piece. It's quite remarkable, as I'm sure you know. I suppose it should come as no surprise that she is exquisitely gifted, but I understand she choreographed the piece as well, which is extraordinary. You must be so proud of her. I'm sure her father would have been."

"Veronika? The Saint-Saens?" Mrs. Popova was clearly taken aback by this turn of events. "You saw her bird dance?"

"Saw it and loved it. My anonymous source also told me that you might be looking to transfer Veronika from Vaganova to another institution. I've come, in all humility, to invite Veronika to study with us at Kannon. Vaganova is unparalleled, of course, when it comes to classical tradition. But after watching your daughter dance, I suspect that our Academy might be a better fit for her creative, experimental style. We are, of course, prepared to offer her a full scholarship. It would be such an honor to have her! And I must admit, now that I've met you in person, the idea of working side by side with you to nurture her talent is most appealing." He caught her gaze and then dropped his eyes.

Mrs. Popova was silent for a moment, taking this all in.

"Oh dear Madam, have I been too forward? I'm not usually so awkward in these situations, but I find myself quite distracted by your charming presence. Forgive me. I'll let myself out and give you time to think about this. Here's my card. Please call me when you've had time to consider my invitation."

He stood and turned to leave, but Mrs. Popova rose hurriedly to stop him.

"Oh, no. Please don't go just yet. We have so much to talk about, and you haven't finished your tea! I was startled, as I hadn't thought of Kannon for Veronika. But now that you present yourself—I mean the school, of course—so kindly and generously, I find I'm quite inclined to place my gifted daughter in your care. She's in her room. Let me call her."

Nika, in her bedroom down the hall, heard her mother's voice, dripping with honey. "Veronika, my precious, please come here. We have a guest who would like to meet you!"

Several weeks later, Chorie found this e-mail message waiting for her:

Dear Chorie,
I was so sad when I went to the Shelter and Doc told me you'd gone back to Greece. I hope it wasn't bad news that sent

you home early. I miss you. I have so much to tell you!

The most amazing thing happened! Just as they were about to kick me out of Vaganova, someone sent Kannon Dance a video of my audition. Do you know Kannon? It's a wonderful school, but not nearly as traditional as the Vaganova. The Director was so impressed that he came to visit Mother and offered me a scholarship to study there! I started the next week and I love it so much! I'm learning about choreography, as well as performance, and they're letting me dance the way that makes me happy! I have a lot to learn about modern dance, but I'll work hard. And now I can work to make myself proud, since they don't expect me to be a copy of my father.

What I still can't believe is that Mother let this happen! I never thought she'd "lower herself" to consider a modern school—even one as good as Kannon. Maybe she really **was** listening and figuring out that I'm not like Papa. Though honestly, I think it has more to do with Mr. Borodin, the Director at Kannon. They've been spending a lot of time together. He has a huge crush on her, and she's soaking up the attention like a sponge in a puddle. It's kind of funny and kind of annoying, but I'm not complaining!

Here's the best part! I'm working on a dance to the "Kangaroos" piece from Carnival of the Animals. I want to train the new rabbit at the Shelter to dance it with me. I know he's not a kangaroo, but he's really smart and the music suits him! And Doc agreed that when I have several dances ready, I can do a recital or make a video to raise money for the Shelter.

Hey, it's not fifty dancing elephants, but it's a start!

Please write back!

Your bird-brained dance partner, Nika

Footnotes

1. Ballet terms are used in this story. A *pirouette* is a type of spin, *arabesque* describes a dancer supported on one leg with the other extended behind, a *demi-plie* is a continuous, partial bending of the knees, and in a *relevé*, the dancer rises to

balance on one or both feet with heels off the floor.

2. Piroshka are meat-filled pastries; borscht is a beet-based soup that can be served hot or cold.

3. Schubert, Leda. *Ballet of the Elephants.* Roaring Book Press, 2006.

4. *Carnival of the Animals* is a musical suite of fourteen movements, written in 1886 by the French composer, Camille Saint-Saens. Each movement pays humorous tribute to a different animal or group of animals.

5. Harpies were ugly, ill-tempered monsters, half bird and half woman, whom the gods used to torment their enemies.

6. Aphrodite was the Greek goddess of love, famous for her own romantic exploits and her fondness for using love potions to inflict passion on unlikely or unsuspecting gods, goddesses, and humans.

CHAPTER 10
CALLIOPE'S MISSION: FLAP, FLAP, CLAP!

Calliope, as Muse of heroes and heroic poetry, your expertise involves both epic storytelling and those rare qualities and acts of heroism that epic poems celebrate. There's a young man in Brazil with a serious case of hero-worship who has set himself up for painful disappointment. Your mission is to help him grow in his understanding of true heroes and find genuine heroism, around and within himself, to inspire stories worth recording and celebrating.

Tres Rios, Brazil

"Fa-bio! Fa-bio! Fa-bio!"

Luis and his brother Victor pumped their fists and chanted with the crowd on the television, as their favorite football [1] star, Fabio Costa, made his third hat trick [2] of the season. Costa had already led his team to a World Cup championship and was the darling of Brazilian football. For that matter, football fans all over the world were under his spell. Not only was he amazing on the field, Costa was also tall, handsome, and charismatic—a showman, as well as an athlete. Opposing teams feared him and the camera loved him almost as much as the star-struck brothers did. Certainly, no star shone brighter in the eyes of Luis and Victor, who never missed a game on TV or a chance to cheer for their hero.

But much more than a shared idol bonded Luis and Victor. Their father, an officer in the Brazilian Navy, was stationed in Haiti with the United Nations peacekeeping force and was rarely home. That made the twelve- and fifteen-year-old brothers "men of the house." It was a role they took seriously. They had to! Sharing their home in the small Brazilian city of Tres Rios with their mother and two little sisters wasn't always easy. It made them natural allies.

They both had their father's amber eyes and coarse, dark hair. Though Luis was younger, people often mistook him for the older of the two. Victor had been born with Escalante's Syndrome [3]. Despite being tall for his age, his shyness, long face, large ears, halting speech, and limited understanding made him seem childlike and vulnerable. Luis had always been Victor's best friend and protector. Just the week before, at a football game, a boy on the opposing team had seen Victor flapping his hands, as some people with Escalantes do when they get excited, and asked him, with a sneer, if he was trying to fly. Luis had stepped between them, moved in close with fists clenched and eyes narrowed, and asked if he was looking for a fight. The boy had backed down, mumbling something about "not being able to take a joke." Anyone who picked on Victor had to answer to Luis!

The brothers relived Costa's scoring plays the next day, as they walked home from football practice, where Luis played defense and Victor served as unofficial team manager. Their mother greeted them at the door, excitement making her dark eyes sparkle.

"Boys! You won't believe this! Guess what I found out at my Escalante's support group today! Never mind; you'll never guess! Look at this!"

She held up a flyer. Two words jumped out of the text and made Luis's heart pound—"Escalante's" and "Costa."

"What?"

He grabbed the paper and forced himself to read from beginning to end. Could this be right? It said that Fabio Costa, himself, would play in an exhibition game in Rio de Janeiro. The game would be part of a charity event, raising money for the Fraxa Research Foundation, the international organization looking for treatments for Escalante's Syndrome. The game would take place at Maracana Stadium in Rio, in two months. And... *Really?* The sponsors were holding an essay contest for young people from around the state with an interest in the Syndrome. Winners would get two tickets for the game and a rally for the Fraxa Foundation the night before, where they would meet Costa in person!

"Luis, you have to enter! This is perfect for you! This event will draw the whole country's attention to Escalante's research, and you could be part of it! You'll try, won't you?"

"Of course, I'll try! I'm not that good at essays, but I can't pass this up. What do you think, Vic? Will you help me write it?"

"Will we get to see Costa play?"

"Maybe, Vic. What do you say?"

"Yes! Let's start right now!"

The weeks after Luis submitted his essay seemed to crawl by. Each day, Luis and Victor raced to check the mail, looking for word on the contest. So Luis was totally unprepared when the news came in a phone call to Mama.

"Luis, Victor!" Mama shouted. "That was Patricia, from the Escalante's group. You were chosen! You're going to Rio for the benefit game! She said that three others from our area were also chosen. The group will send you in a bus, provide chaperones, and pay for you to stay in a hotel!"

The details were lost on Luis, as he whooped and jumped around the room, grabbing an ecstatic Victor to spin with him in a crazy dance. Luis flapped his hands, in affectionate mimicry of Victor's obsessive gesture, and said, "Flap, flap, **clap**!" In response, Victor held his palms out for the two-handed high-five clap which, combined with the flap, was the brothers' equivalent of a secret handshake. Later, as they celebrated over hot chocolate, they reviewed the details of this dream come true.

"We're really going to see Costa?" asked Victor.

"We really are! You and me, Vic. It'll be great!"

On the day of the rally in Rio de Janeiro, Mama drove Luis past the Nestles factory and to the church where the Escalante's support group met and the bus would be waiting. Luis was nearly jumping out of his skin with excitement.

"I wish Vic could come with me today," he said, reining in his enthusiasm for a moment.

"I know, *meu filho* [4]. I wish so, too. But you know Victor doesn't do well in crowds and unfamiliar situations. It would be too hard on both of you. He'll do much better driving over with the girls and me tomorrow and sitting with us at the game. But he's so proud of you, Luis. And so am I, for giving him this chance."

"Thanks, Mama. I still can hardly believe that I'm going to meet Fabio Costa in person! I just hope Victor can meet him, too, tomorrow."

In the parking lot, a group gathered around the bus, where kids were checking in with parents or assigned chaperones. Luis and a boy from a neighboring town were directed to a young woman of medium height and build, with dark hair and violet eyes, wearing a no-nonsense red and gray pantsuit. She looked to be in her early twenties, but her confident, take-charge manner made it clear she claimed authority over the two young travelers. "I'm Calliope," she announced, thrusting a hand out to each boy in turn. "Call me Calli. I work with the Fraxa Foundation's partner in Rio. And you are...?" She pulled out a small notebook and pen and logged in the boys' names, cell phone numbers, and suitcases—all business. "Put your bags in the luggage compartment. I'll meet you on the bus. We'll go over some rules for the trip."

Luis and Marcos, Callie's other charge, tried to listen attentively as Calli laid out a list of strict rules about what the boys could and couldn't do, while in her care. But they were too excited, and her bossiness made them even more jumpy.

They caught each other's eyes and made faces when she wasn't looking. They were in clear, if unspoken, agreement that they were not going to let Calli dampen their spirits on this best-of-all-possible adventures. And even Calli lightened up a bit, once she'd laid out her expectations.

"Tell me, you two, what's so great about this Fabio Costa? Every kid on the bus, and most of the adults, seem totally in love with this guy. So he's a good athlete. So what?"

Luis blurted out "**Good**?!" at the same time Marcos shouted, "**So what**?" Astounded at her ignorance, they proceeded to educate her by taking turns reciting every impressive statistic and recounting every stellar moment of Fabio Costa's meteoric career, to date.

"OK! I get it! You'd think this guy was some kind of demigod [5], the way you two talk! Here's what I want to know. Is he as amazing off the field as he is on it?"

"He's doing this benefit game, isn't he? That makes him even cooler, if you ask me," replied Luis.

"Well, I can't argue with that. It's a pretty great thing to do. And speaking of the benefit, tell me about your essays. Why are you interested in Escalante's Syndrome?"

Marcos mentioned a neighbor he'd grown up with, who had mild symptoms of Escalante's. But it was clear he was more interested in meeting Costa than in the Syndrome. He nodded off to sleep as Calli and Luis chatted. Luis was eager to talk about his brother and about living with Escalante's. He spoke freely, with a frankness that was inappropriate in most situations. He was so intent that he forgot to notice the familiar landmarks and big-city bustle that usually seemed so exciting, compared to the relative tameness of Tres Rios—glimpses of the Christ the Redeemer statue; car horns sounding; conflicting scents of salt air, fresh fruits, and exhaust fumes.

"Victor's a great guy, you know? But sometimes I wish he could be more like a real big brother. We have a good time, but there are so many things he can't do with me, that are too hard or make him upset."

"Like what things?" Calli asked.

"He can't really play football with me, and he can't help me with my homework, like my best friend's big sister does.

We can watch TV together and play some games. But anything complicated, like chess or the computer and video games I like, is too hard. He gets frustrated. And he doesn't read too well, so he doesn't like to play games or do things that need much reading."

Calli could hear the wistfulness in Luis's voice. Her usual brusqueness faded and she felt a pang of sympathy. "What's the hardest part for you, having Victor as your brother?"

"That's easy. Having to look out for him all the time. It really makes me mad when people pick on him and I'm glad to chase them off or shut them up. There's this one guy, Renaldo, who's always laughing at him and saying mean things. He doesn't do it around me anymore, after I stood up to him a couple of times—even hit him once. But sometimes I get tired—you know?—of always having part of my brain tuned in for anything that might hurt him. I want to protect him; it's just hard sometimes."

"Sounds like Victor's lucky to have you for a brother."

"I guess. But I feel lucky, too, most of the time. I don't know anybody more loyal or cheerful than Vic, even though people can be so mean and he gets so frustrated. I figure it's lots harder to **be** Vic than to watch out for him."

Calli looked around the bus and saw a girl a bit younger than Luis, giggling and flapping her hands excitedly.

"Does Victor do that a lot? The hand flapping thing?" she asked.

"He used to do it all the time. But then we sort of made a game of it. When he starts to flap, I say "Flap, flap, **clap**!" and hold up my hands, like this." He demonstrated, palms out. "He slaps my hands with his, like a double high-five. It's sort of our thing. After that, he can usually stop flapping."

The bus wound its way through congested traffic, past open-air markets and Maracana Stadium, and into the hotel parking lot. As it slowed, kids woke up and perked up, wondering if Fabio would be there to greet them. Instead, an older woman with a clipboard, who introduced herself as Senhora [6] Almeida, greeted them. To the chorus of questions about Costa, she replied, "He'd hoped to be here, but something must have come up. He has a very busy schedule, you know." Her words were cheerful, but Calli noticed a different emotion in her eyes—more like annoyance or disappointment. The woman checked the children off her list and sent them into the lobby with a promise that they, and the other winners from around the state, would meet the football star at the rally that evening. Frowning, Calli followed the boys into the lobby.

Later that evening, in the hotel ballroom, an excited crowd of Fabio fans from eight to eighty waited for their hero to appear and kick off the rally. They all wore T-shirts in bright colors, sporting the slogan *F. C. for Escalante's Research*. As Calli looked around the room, she saw many people whose appearance and mannerisms suggested Escalante's Syndrome. Others showed no such signs. In some cases, she couldn't be sure by looking. One young girl got upset, started to shout and cry, and had to be led from the room. Not one person, Calli noticed, gave her behavior more than a brief, sympathetic glance. *These people are so understanding,* she thought, surprised and impressed. *I don't think anyone behaving that way at a banquet back home would be treated as well. I wonder, if I hadn't learned about this condition, would I be so kind? It's so easy to laugh at people, without even wondering why they do what they do.*

Anticipation built in the room, as time went by. Finally, Senhora Almeida, who had greeted the bus, walked to the podium.

"Welcome, all of you, to this benefit event to support research on treatments for Escalante's Syndrome. I know that this condition affects every person in this room. Fraxa Research Foundation, along with Rio's Fragile X Association [7], celebrates all of you—those living with the Syndrome and those who love and support them. We'll talk more later about Fraxa's exciting and promising research projects. But I know you're all eager to meet our featured guest, our honored partner in this event, and perhaps the greatest all-around player in football today. So here, without further delay, is Fabio Costa!"

The crowd began chanting, "Fa-bio! Fa-bio! Fa-bio!" as

the dashing, well-muscled athlete jogged onto the stage and took a bow. He waved and pranced around as the crowd applauded and cheered, thrilled to meet their hero at last. When the noise finally tapered off, Fabio picked up the microphone.

"Ola, all you football fans! I'm glad to be here tonight to see you and support this worthy cause. I'll be even happier to hit Maracana Stadium tomorrow, with a couple of my teammates, to beat the pants off these Foundation folks and raise lots of money for their work!"

Again, wild cheering and clapping from the crowd.

"I'll be around for pictures after the game, while these guys…," he pointed at the Fraxa and local foundation staffers at the front of the crowd, "are collapsing in the locker room and recovering from humiliating defeat! See you all there!"

Fabio jogged off the stage and out the side door of the ballroom, to another round of cheers and applause. The evening's host, who had barely gotten to her chair and settled, looked startled as she stood again and headed back to the podium. She laughed a bit nervously.

"It seems that Senhor Costa is a man of few words! But we all know he more than makes up for it in action on the football field! I'm relieved to say that I'm not on the brave, or maybe foolish, team that will face him there tomorrow!"

The crowd, also startled to see their champion come and go so quickly, managed to laugh appreciatively.

"Now, let's get on with our program. We'll introduce the brave souls who **are** on the team that will face Fabio tomorrow, hear some comments from the Director of the local Fragile X Association, and then invite you to visit displays around the room and talk to the researchers about their projects. I think you'll be encouraged."

Calli, who couldn't help being impressed with Fabio's obvious charm, quickly returned to skepticism as she looked around the room. The elation of a few moments before had melted into a general air of confusion and disappointment. Irritation rose in her, as she thought about his failure to show up to greet the bus and his brief, almost dismissive, comments to a bunch of innocent young people so ready to adore him.

She looked at Luis and couldn't read his expression.

After the speeches, she asked, "So what are you thinking, Luis? Is he as great as you expected?"

"I guess so. I don't know. It was just over so quickly. I don't know exactly what I expected, but… something more."

"It does seem like a let-down, after you all looked forward to him so much."

"But I know he's busy, training and all. I'm sure he'll be great at the game tomorrow. Maybe Victor and I can get our picture taken with him…." His voice trailed off.

"I hope so, Luis. I really hope so. For now, why don't you and Marcos go get some punch and see what the researchers are up to? I'll be back in a few minutes. Restroom, you know."

Calliope left the ballroom, her anger growing by the minute. *Who is Fabio Costa, anyway, to treat his fans as though they aren't worth his time? I don't like him and I don't trust him, not for a minute! Why did he run off like that? Where does he have to go that's more important than this room full of people who are crazy about him? I'd like to ask him that to his face! And I would, if I didn't have to stay here and keep an eye on Luis and Marcos. Stay focused,* she reminded herself. *I'm here to help Luis.*

Calli fumed as she found her way to an outside door. Maybe some fresh air would help. But the more she thought, the angrier she got. *The nerve of this guy! How I'd love to give him a piece of my mind….*

Wait a minute—maybe a sister could help! I'd rather handle him myself, but after all, I've spent enough time already trying to rescue the others' missions. They owe me! Let's see… I've already bailed out Erato and Euterpe, but neither of them has the guts to deal with someone like Fabio Costa. Besides, they're probably both mad at me. Maybe Polyhymnia. She's not likely to be impressed with Costa's celebrity, and I can count on her to follow instructions.

Calli called Polly with the finger-tapping code. Polly joined her just outside the hotel entrance.

"Hi, Calli. This is a surprise! Don't tell me you need help with your mission! And you called me? What's up? What can I do?"

"I only need help because I can't be two places at once, and Mother's arranged it so that I'm responsible for a couple of kids here at the hotel. I need someone to find out about this aggravating celebrity who's passing himself off as a hero around here. Here's the situation...."

Calli brought Polly up to date, sparing no detail in her description of Costa's reputation and contrasting behavior.

"OK, I get it. Spy on the jerk. Find out what he's really made of, when he thinks no one's looking. Tracking him should be simple enough—just follow the paparazzi! "

"Right. Check him out and let me know what you learn. I'll be right here, waiting. Be quick about it!"

"I'll see what I can do. I hope it is quick, though. I'm at a kind of sensitive place in my own mission." She disappeared.

Across the city, at an upscale, exclusive nightclub, Polly spotted the man her sister had described, sitting in a booth with another athletic-looking man and two glamorous women. *That's got to be him,* she thought. *As mortals go, they look like "the beautiful people" to me.* She ducked out long enough to change into waitress attire and returned, unobtrusively busying herself tidying up nearby tables. She scanned the room for paparazzi, but saw only one man who looked the part. He stood in a corner looking busy on his cell phone, but he had placed himself strategically for best view of Costa's table and kept shooting furtive glances in that direction. If he was looking for a scoop, he didn't have long to wait. The conversation took an interesting turn.

Fabio shouted in Polly's direction, "Hey, are you deaf? What does it take to get some service over here? My friends and I are thirsty! You got something better to do?"

Polly answered through gritted teeth, "No, senhor. I'll be with you in just a minute." She continued wiping the table and listening.

"So, Fabio, what are you doing in town, anyway? I heard Sophia was going on holiday in Barbados. And you're here, off season, doing some lame charity event? You may be the hottest catch in all of Brazil, amigo, but even you might want to think twice about leaving Sophia alone too much!"

"Crazy, isn't it? I'm only doing this stupid benefit because my agent says I should line up more sponsors and product endorsement deals, and this will make me look like a real sweetheart. Imagine! I could be on the beach right now. Instead I'm here, expected to hang out with a bunch of flapping retard freaks, and pretend I like it, at that!"

Polly almost dropped the empty glass in her hand. She glanced at the man on the phone. His eyes widened and his jaw dropped. Yes, he'd clearly heard what she heard. She watched his expression change from shock, to horror, to something like glee. Within seconds, he was tapping on his phone with purposeful intent. Polly worked her way to his corner and asked, in the tone of a co-conspirator, "Did you get all that?"

The man looked surprised, then wary. "You bet. You?"

"Oh, I got it alright. But you can have the scoop, as long as you promise that the rest of the world will get it right away!"

"Already done. Twitter should be starting to tweet away about now."

"Good. Then there's only one thing left for me to do."

Polly moved back across the room, picking up a nearly full glass left on an unoccupied table. She approached Costa and, without even the pretense of stumbling, threw the drink in his face. She strode out the door before he could overcome his shock and come after her.

The reception at the hotel continued, with a subdued buzz. Small groups gathered around the research exhibits, where talk was positive and animated. But most of the young people wandered aimlessly or stood with other kids in twos and threes, quietly comparing notes on their hopes for the event and their disappointment so far. Calli gave up trying to draw out Luis and Marcos, and paced a corner of the room. Suddenly, Polly ran toward her, grinning broadly.

"Well?" Calli asked. "Why the grin? What did you find out?"

"When you're right, you're right, Sis. Turns out Narcissus [8] has nothing on this guy!"

"What? Tell me. How can we use it to show him up for the

jackass he is?"

"Oh, we're way past figuring out how to use it! It's done, and you didn't really need me at all. But it was fun…."

She described the scene at the nightclub.

"Now, just watch and listen. Phones should be buzzing anytime now."

Sure enough, adults and kids around the room were pulling cell phones from cases, purses, and pockets. Twitter users were directed to a YouTube video, showing the whole ugly scene. Non-Twitter users got text messages from friends. The video was going viral and Fabio Costa would have nowhere to hide.

"I know I shouldn't be happy," Polly said guiltily, after watching the damning video. "What he said is going to hurt lots of people, whether they looked up to him or not."

"I'd love to punch him right in his perfect nose," replied Calli, "In fact, I can think of a few more creative things I'd like to do to him, like…"

"Calli, don't even think about it! You know Mother wouldn't approve. Besides, your mission is about your kid, not Costa."

"Unfortunately, you're right. Though I'd give anything to have been the one to throw that drink in his smug face! Still, well done!" Calli said, looking on her sister with newfound respect. "I wouldn't have thought you had it in you! I only told you to find out about him, but I'm glad you made the moment count. Now, the question is how Luis and the rest here are going to take it and how I can use it to finish my mission."

"You'll figure it out. I've got to go."

"Thanks!" Calli called after her, with uncharacteristic admiration. "See you soon, back home."

Meanwhile, the mood in the ballroom was rapidly shifting from somber to stunned. People moved around, sharing the shocking news via phones or conversation. First, collective numbness and unbelief; then increasing animation and scurrying. People were peeling off their event T-shirts, bearing tribute to the traitorous "F.C.," and tossing them on the floor. Calli saw Senhora Almeida gather a group of adults for a lively, whispered consultation.

Calli spotted Luis and Marcos in the crowd and made her way to them. Marcos was kicking at nothing on the floor; Luis was staring into space. Tears formed in his eyes.

"Calli, did you hear? Do you believe it? Could it be some sort of trick to make him look bad?"

"I did hear and I do believe it. It's no trick, Luis. It's sad, but sometimes 'heroes' turn out not to be the people you thought they were. Costa's probably so stuck on himself he doesn't even realize how much pain he's caused."

"Sad? It's not sad, it's horrible! Unforgivable! Who does he think he is? Do you know what this will do to Victor?" With Victor filling his mind, Luis reacted out of habit when an older boy with Escalante's Syndrome walked by, agitatedly flapping his hands. Luis held his own palms up, in front of his neon green *F.C. for Escalante's Research* T-shirt, for the expected clap, then dropped them dejectedly when it didn't come.

Calli's eyes flashed with the seed of an idea. "Wait, Luis. What's that thing you and Victor do? Show me again! Did you say you and Vic say, 'Flap, flap, **clap**!' when you do that?"

Luis nodded, confused.

Calli raised her eyebrows. "Think about what you do there. You take that strange-looking flap of Escalante's and turn it into something like encouragement, or even applause. I think I know something you can do to take some attention away from Costa and put it back on the people he's hurt." She pulled a marker out of her pocket and told Luis to stand still. Below the *F* for Fabio, she added letters to spell "Flap, flap." She turned the *C* beside the *F* into "**Clap**!"

Marcos and others around them took an interest. When Calli explained the phrase, where it came from, and what it meant, a few began to try it out and then ask to borrow the marker.

Screeching feedback from the microphone drew everyone's eyes to the front of the room. Senhora Almeida stood at the podium, calling for attention. The crowd hushed, all eyes on her.

What can she possibly say? wondered Calli, and surprised herself by feeling rather sorry for the woman.

"Thank you for your attention. I'm sure, by now, most of

you have seen the disturbing video that's circulating. We, the staff of the Fragile X Association and sponsors of this event are, like you, shocked and saddened by what we've seen and heard. First, we must be very clear that Senhor Costa does **not** speak for any of us or, I'd bet, anyone else in this room. We, like you, feel betrayed by his despicable behavior. We hold all people struggling with Escalante's and its effects in the highest respect. We want to go on record as officially condemning Senhor Costa's words. We believe that people of conscience everywhere, including many in the football world, will agree and join us in that condemnation.

"That being said, it's obvious that we cannot allow Senhor Costa to have any further role in this event. For that reason, we're forced to cancel tomorrow's exhibition game and hope that the many generous people who were considering supporting our cause will find it in their hearts to do so, in spite of this unfortunate turn of events. We're so sorry for the disappointment, and worse, that all of this has caused."

The room was silent. No one knew what to say or do. Drinking punch, mingling, and showing enthusiasm for new, unproven treatments seemed impossible. Then Calli's voice rose, strong and commanding in the quiet.

"Wait, everyone, wait! There's someone with me who has something to show you. It might cheer you up." She grabbed Luis's hand and started moving toward the stage.

"What, me? No, Calli, I don't know what to say. I can't..."

Calli ignored him and kept pulling. He had no choice but to move with her. She dragged him up the steps and to the podium.

"Hi, everybody. This is Luis. His brother has Escalante's Syndrome and he has something to show you that might make you feel better. It's a way to write Costas out of this event and substitute something positive. Tell them, Luis."

Luis found himself thrust in front of the microphone. "Uh, hi. I'm Luis. I guess she already said that. Sorry." Luis's face flamed and his voice cracked with nervousness. He gulped and, because there seemed nothing else to do, continued. "It's really not a big thing. It's just this thing my brother Victor and I do. When he flaps his hands, you know, like some of you do, I say, 'Flap, flap, **clap**!' and hold up my hands like this." He demonstrated. "Then he slaps them, like a high-five clap." He turned to Calli, who slapped his palms with her own. "Victor doesn't like it when he flaps, so he likes this because it helps him stop. But mainly, he likes it because he knows I'm not making fun of him. It's sort of like clapping for him—a way to show him I love him just the way he is. Then Calli, here, saw that the letters on our T-shirts could stand for 'Flap, flap, **clap**!' instead of Fabio Costa, see? And some of us thought that was kind of cool. So we did it. You could, too."

Luis started to step away from the microphone. Small bursts of applause began to break out around the room. They spread, until the whole crowd was clapping. Senhora Almeida and her coworkers went scrambling for marking pens to pass around the crowd. Luis watched as smiles broke out everywhere he looked. It emboldened him. He stepped back to the microphone.

"Oh, and one more thing. Why do we have to cancel the game tomorrow? My brother's coming, and my mom and sisters, and they want to watch a game! Now I'm no Fabio Costa, and after tonight, I don't want to be anything like him. I'm only an OK footballer, and I've never made a hat trick in my life. But I love the game and I love my brother. I'm willing to play against anybody tomorrow, and I'll bet there's at least a team's worth of others here that feel the same way, right?"

Many voice shouted, "Right!"

Luis continued. "If we totally embarrass ourselves, well, at least we showed that phony 'hero' that he can't keep us down. And if the people with the money can't support us without him, then I guess we'll just have to manage without them. So what do you say? Have we got a game?"

Luis and Calli beamed, as the crowd roared and cheered. Senhor Almeida approached the podium and honored Luis with applause and a smile.

Above the din, she announced, "The sponsors are unanimous. We have a game! Same time, same place. Thanks to you, young man, for saving the day for all of us! See you all at Maracana Stadium tomorrow!"

Back home in Tres Rios the next evening, Luis and Victor hopped around the kitchen and "flap, flap, clapped," too excited to sit, while their mother read aloud the column on the front page of the sports section of Rio's *O Globo* newspaper:

Escalante's Syndrome's New Hero

Shouting, cheering fans filled Maracana Stadium this morning, as a young hero led his team to victory in an exhibition football game to benefit Escalante's Syndrome research.

No surprise there. That's the story we expected to print today, based on plans for the event. But the game was not quite what everyone expected, and the hero was definitely not the one originally scheduled to appear! Instead of Fabio Costa, an unlikely young hero arose from the Escalante's benefit attendees. Luis Rocha, twelve- year-old resident of Tres Rios, whose brother has Escalante's Syndrome, came out of nowhere, it seemed, to save the whole event from disaster. Here's how it happened.

After Costa appeared briefly at the opening reception for the Escalante's charity event, a journalist recorded him making insulting comments about his young fans with Escalante's. The video went viral, disgracing the popular athlete in a most public way. Benefit planners saw no alternative but to cancel the game, abandoning their goal to raise a million Brazilian Reals for Escalante's research. But young Luis refused to let his former hero's inexcusable behavior ruin the event. He took to the stage, rallied the shocked and disappointed crowd, and recruited a team of event participants, including two with Escalante's Syndrome, to play against event sponsors and planners in Costa's place.

It was, perhaps, not the brilliant display of football skills Costa would have provided. Rocha's team of youngsters claimed a 7-to-6 victory over their older opponents. But it was a touching and inspiring display of courage and character, as evidenced by donations totaling nearly 1.4 million Reals!

This poem, submitted anonymously to O Globo *shortly after the game, seems like the perfect way to end today's column:*

For Luis, Heartfelt Hero
Sweet Calliope, guide my pen
As I recount the mighty deeds
Of one, unheralded, who arose
To serve his peers in time of need.

While in pursuit of righteous cause,
The lauded champion of the day
Did fail the trusting throng with words
Unkind, revealing feet of clay.

Yet from the company of the wronged,
One humbly, bravely, spoke of dreams
And victories that must be won,
For loved ones held in high esteem.

Then from his words the throng took heart
And met the challenge on the field,
Thus making clear to one and all
That heartfelt heroes never yield.
- Anonymous

Footnotes
1. What we, in the USA, call soccer is called football in Brazil, and in much of the world.
2. When a player scores three goals in a single game, it's called a hat trick.
3. Escalante's syndrome, also called Fragile X or Martin-Bell Syndrome, is a genetic syndrome that affects about 1 in 3600 boys and 1 in 5000 girls around the world—estimates vary. It can produce physical characteristics like a long face, large forehead, large ears, and flat feet; behaviors like hand-flapping, hyperactivity, and social anxiety; and developmental disabilities like mental retardation, speech problems, and autism.
4. "My son" in Portuguese, the language spoken in Brazil.

5. In Greek mythology, demigods are the children of a god and a mortal, so literally "half gods." They often have superhuman abilities.

6. *Senhora* is Portuguese for "Mrs." Likewise, *Senhor* is used for "Mr. "

7. Fraxa Research Foundation, the leading international organization working on new treatments for Fragile X syndrome, cooperates with similar local and national organizations. The Associacao X Fragil do Brasil (Fragile X Association of Brazil) is one such organization.

8. Narcissus, in Greek mythology, was the son of a river god and a nymph. He was so proud of his own attractiveness that he could love no one but himself. In fact, he fell in love with his reflection in a pool and wasted away, worshipping his own beauty! To this day the term *narcissism* refers to a person who is so impressed with himself that no one else matters.

CHAPTER 11

AFTER

One by one, as they finished their missions, the Muses returned home to Mount Helicon. They were confined to their individual suites until the last sister arrived, which was no hardship—their quarters were spacious and lavish, as befitted goddesses of their stature. They had every comfort, yet not one could feel comfortable while they waited. When would the last Muse return? Had they all completed their missions successfully? Would they celebrate with pear sorbet or lose that heavenly pleasure forever? They were left to reflect, ponder, and hope.

Finally, the summons came. Each sister received an invitation to join her mother and sisters in the Music Hall. Each sister stepped from her private suite into the corridor, feeling both eager and anxious. Seeing each other for the first time since their missions, some sisters hugged excitedly. Some kept to themselves. Some glared at each other. They proceeded toward the Music Hall in twos and threes, whispering, giggling, or staring straight ahead.

When they reached the Hall, a large table awaited them, with nine chairs around and Mnemosyne's elaborate throne at the head. It was empty. The sisters sat and looked at each other, nervous as

Theseus going into the labyrinth [1].

The rest jumped when Calliope began speaking. "Well? Why are we whispering? We're all back, so that means our missions are finished. Did you all succeed? Erato, did you manage to redirect your young poet's affections, so he could finally wise up? Euterpe—or should I say 'Sunny?'—did your girl with the dreadful voice get straightened out? As for me, I'm quite satisfied with my young charge. With my guidance, he rose to the occasion and proved himself quite the hero."

"Don't forget, Calli," Polly spoke up from the end of the table, "you had a little help. I have to say, I very much enjoyed giving that egotistical football jerk a little of what was coming to him!"

"I give you full credit. You surprised me," Calli responded. "I didn't think you had it in you to let him have it the way you did. You've got some guts!"

"That's all fine, you two," Urania protested, "but what if Mother takes it out on all of us that **some** didn't follow the rules? I can't believe how closely she was watching us, and now I hear that Terpsichore and Erato conjured up a love potion to help Chorie's girl get what she wanted. I swear, if I lose my pear sorbet forever because you just **had** to resort to magic…"

The buzzing ceased abruptly, when Mnemosyne strode into the hall and made her way to the head of the table.

"My darling daughters, welcome home! What a joy to see you all again, bursting with your recent accomplishments! If I say so myself, my plan worked beautifully, and I've had a nice, **mostly** peaceful respite—not to mention that some of your missions proved to be highly entertaining! I'd like to offer a few observations, if I may. And of course, I may." she chuckled. "It's my plan, after all!"

"First, Polyhymnia. You got a bit carried away with your cover story. You caused me some concern, as you almost lost sight of your mission. But I enjoyed watching you embrace your task. You showed resourcefulness and, in the end, you accomplished more than I expected of you. Not only did you complete your specific task with distinction, but you managed to broaden another young Australian's world, and perhaps your own experience, as well. Well done!"

Polly beamed with relief and pleasure. She **had** gained valuable experience and real friends, though who knew if she'd ever see them again. Her smile faded to a sigh.

"Now, Euterpe and Erato, I know you are both unhappy with Calliope's role in your missions. Erato, you must remember that

Calliope was doing my bidding when I sent her to you. I trust you will not hold that against her. Euterpe, you know Calliope can be... headstrong. Yet you called on her to aid you. Did you not expect her to behave like herself? And in the end, your mission turned out beautifully for everyone, don't you agree? So, no hard feelings. I insist.

Erato and Euterpe frowned and then nodded, appeased, if not content.

"Melpomene, you came dangerously close to revealing your identity. But you restrained yourself and got the job done.

"Urania, you nearly got yourself fired from the role you'd chosen to complete your mission! What would you have done then, I wonder. You took a big chance, confiding something near the truth to your young scientist. But it paid off, and your young man benefited from it.

"Next, Thalia. You did an excellent job of winning the trust of your young subject, but wouldn't you agree that an important element of your success was good advice from Clio at a crucial moment in the process?"

Thalia smiled, stood, and made a little bow in Clio's direction. "Yes, Mother, I agree. That bit of reverse psychology did the trick. Thank you, Clio."

Mother continued.

"Urania, you had another tense moment, when you could have ruined things for everyone by tasting the cook's version of pear sorbet. But you deserve credit for recognizing the danger and grabbing the lifeline I offered you. Crisis nicely averted, dear.

"That brings us back to you, Erato and you, Terpsichore," Mnemosyne continued, fixing pointed glances on each as she pronounced her name.

The two sisters, sitting side by side, grasped each other's hands nervously. There was silence around the table.

"Really, girls, a love potion? Such a cliché! And I thought I'd been clear about avoiding magic in your personal interactions." Mother frowned at the girls, causing little gasps around the table. She held the frown as long as she could. The anxiety on her daughters' faces was amusing. But she relented, breaking into a gentle laugh. "Still, you caught me on a tiny technicality. I could, I suppose, hold you to the spirit of the rule rather than the letter, but your reasoning was rather clever and the results superb! So how could I object? At worst, a victimless crime that served a greater purpose."

Relief flooded the faces of the sisters in question.

Mnemosyne looked out at the nine pairs of violet eyes, fixed on her with hope and anticipation. She met each pair around the table, in turn.

"So. I'm proud of you all! You used your own and each others' strengths to serve your calling and inspire young mortals. They are all better for it, and so, I believe, are you. Now, your reward."

She clapped her hands sharply, twice. Athena herself led a procession of servers, each carrying a covered silver tray. Athena herself took each tray and set it before a Muse, removing each silver lid with a flourish. Nine pairs of violet eyes lit up over nine delighted smiles. Athena served Mnemosyne, and last, herself, as an extra chair was brought to the table. Eleven silver spoons carried the divine concoction from tray to lips. Eleven blissful sighs rose at first taste. Yes, eleven. Athena herself had to acknowledge that it really was that delicious!

Clinking spoons and contented murmurs filled the room as all eleven women lost themselves in the pleasure of this most delectable of treats. But suddenly, Thalia set down her spoon and looked at Mnemosyne wistfully.

"What is it, Thalia? Aren't your going to finish your sorbet?"

"I will, Mother. It's just as wonderful as I remembered. But I can't help thinking about Timothy. I wish he could taste this, too. It's so much better than that bland, mushy stuff they serve as frozen dessert. He would love it."

Euterpe agreed. "Lily was so miserable the last time I saw her. I know things have worked out well for her, but I wish she could have this pleasure, too, to make up for some of the pain she had to go through."

Urania chimed in. "And Alim's sister's wedding is coming up. I'd hate for them to serve some second-rate imitation of Athena's pear sorbet. Wouldn't it be wonderful if they could have the real thing?"

All eyes turned to Mnemosyne.

"Could we, Mother?"

"Please? Could we?"

Mnemosyne raised her hands against their pleading.

"Really girls? Do you think the mortal world is ready for such riches? You realize, I hope, that none of these humans could ever be content with ordinary desserts, after a taste of Athena's. Is that truly what you want for them? To raise their expectations to such impossible heights?"

"**Yes!**" the Muses shouted in unison.

"Well, I may be sorry. But it's a generous impulse, and I never could refuse you when you look at me with those eyes. So be it!" She sent Athena off to the kitchen and summoned Hermes, half brother of the Muses and messenger of the Gods, to carry out the task.

When Timothy answered the doorbell at his New Prague, Minnesota, farmhouse, he saw a tall, strongly built man, bizarrely dressed in tights, tunic, sandals with wings, and a helmet with wings. Before Timothy could speak, the man handed him a heavy parcel that felt cold to the touch, and left at a trot. Puzzled, Timothy carried the package to the kitchen table. It was addressed to him. Where the return address belonged, there was an odd stamp showing a mountain and the name "Mount Olympus Courier Service." Around the base of the mountain, a ring of nine girls appeared to be dancing.

What the heck..., Timothy thought. But curiosity got the best of him and he tore off the packaging. The silver bowl inside nearly froze his hands. As he lifted the lid, the most delicious smell he could imagine wafted toward him. It overtook the caution and questions in his mind. He grabbed a spoon and dove into a frosty, fruity deliciousness unlike anything he'd tasted before.

One by one, doorbells rang and similar packages were delivered in...

Freetown, Sierra Leone,

Prince Albert, Saskatchewan, Canada,

The Outback near Alice Springs, Northern Territory, Australia,

Florence, Italy,

Tres Rios, Brazil,

Shanghai, The People's Republic of China,

St. Petersburg, Russia,

and finally, Bangalore, India, where the strange messenger left a much larger package, to the bewildered delight of a young woman, soon to be "the happiest bride in all of India."

Meanwhile, back in the Music Hall on Mount Helicon, the Muses took a break from their rehearsal for a banquet in honor of Mnemosyne's upcoming birthday.

Calliope was speaking. "I'm just saying it stands to reason that Mother would give me one of the hardest missions, even knowing that I'd have to keep leaving to help the rest of you."

"You call that **help**?" Euterpe protested. You squashed Lily like a bug!"

Urania joined in. "The hardest mission? Please! You hardly had to do anything, Calli! Polly and the reporter did most of your work for you. But it's true, she certainly couldn't have given you my mission. You'd have lost your temper with Alim and been thrown out of there before you could even get him to remember your name!"

Melpomene objected. "Listen to you, Urania! You got to sit on a roof and stargaze while I coddled along the most annoying whiner in Africa...."

Footnote

1. In order to prove himself worthy to inherit the throne of Athens, Theseus took on a seemingly impossible challenge. King Minos of Crete, a great conqueror, had besieged Athens and set a plague upon its people. He would only lift the plague if Athens agreed to send fourteen young men and women each year to be sacrificed as food for the terrifying half-man, half-bull called the Minotaur, who was imprisoned in an intricate underground labyrinth on Crete. For years, Athens had submitted to the King's demand. But Theseus stepped up and offered himself as one of the youths: he had a plan to defeat the monster and free Athens of this burden. And while, in the end, Theseus had help navigating the maze and managed to kill the Minotaur and emerge a hero, you can imagine his anxiety as he entered the labyrinth to face the fearsome creature.

ATHENA'S HEAVENLY PEAR SORBET

Serves 4

Ingredients:
- 5 small yellow pears, grown on Mount Olympus and ripened to blushing perfection
- 3/4 cup sparkling pear beverage (plus 1/4-1/3 cup for final processing)
- 1/3 cup sugar
- 2" length vanilla bean
- 1 1/2 tablespoons lemon juice

Directions:
1. Peel, core, and slice pears.
2. Mix all ingredients in a saucepan and bring to boil, stirring occasionally. Reduce heat and simmer for about 8 minutes, uncovered, until pears are soft.
3. Cool mixture for 5 minutes in refrigerator.
4. Remove vanilla bean and stir mixture gently.
5. Turn toward Mount Olympus and lift mixture in tribute.
6. In a food processor, process mixture for 2 minutes, until smooth and fine-textured.
7. Pour mixture into a 9" X 13" baking pan and place in freezer for 4-6 hours.
8. Chop frozen mixture into small chunks. Place chunks in food processor and blend again for 1-2 minutes, adding 1/4-1/3 cup sparkling pear beverage, as needed, to make sorbet smooth.
9. Serve in dessert dishes.

ATHENA'S NOTES: If you can't get Mount Olympus pears, substitute the freshest, sweetest yellow pears you can find. I never make this recipe on a cloudy or rainy day; it needs sunshine for perfect flavor. And if Zeus, Hera, or any other Olympians or Titans in residence sneeze before you get the mixture into the freezer, the batch is ruined. Throw it out and start over.

DIANE FINDLAY is an avid lifelong reader with many interests. She holds a Masters Degree in Library Science from the University of Iowa and worked in public libraries in Utah, Antigua, and Iowa for ten years, with emphasis on youth services. Along with reading and children's and young adult literature, her passions include travel and global cultures. She's lived abroad, traveled extensively, worked in international high school student exchange programs, and hosted several international students in her home. As a freelance writer, Diane has a regular column in *LibrarySparks* magazine, and writes various other curriculum and library resource materials. *Bemused* is her first work of fiction.

A country girl at heart, Diane lives with her husband in rural Iowa, where she stays active with family, friends, and her Baha'i community.